MW00682326

Learning To Yearn

Amidst the storms of life

Laurie Kenyon

Learning to Yearn: Amidst the storms of life
Copyright © 2017 Laurie Kenyon

All rights reserved. No part of this book may be reproduced in any manner whatsoever without written permission from the publisher or author except in brief quotations embodied in critical articles or reviews. For information, write Laurie Kenyon, P.O. Box 10, Mitchell, Ontario, Canada N0K 1N0

Scripture quotations: Scripture taken from the New King James Version®. Copyright © 1982 by Thomas Nelson. Used by permission. All rights reserved.

Printed by CreateSpace, An Amazon.com Company

Kenyonspage publications
Box 10, Mitchell, Ontario, Canada, N0K 1N0

ISBN-13: 978-0-9959390-0-4
ISBN-10: 09959390-0-4

Cover design: G G Graphics and Design
graham@gggraphics.ca

Front cover photography: Tim Kenyon
https://www.facebook.com/thenarrowtwistyroad

Back cover photo: Erin Lisa Photography
https://www.facebook.com/erinlisaphotography

DEDICATION

My hope is that this book brings glory to the Lord God who
through the storms of life is teaching me to yearn for Him
alone

For you have been a strength to the poor,
a strength to the needy in his distress, a
refuge from the storm, a shade from the
heat.
Isaiah 25:4

Many are the afflictions of the righteous,
but the Lord delivers him from them all.
Psalm 34:19

CONTENTS

ACKNOWLEDGMENTS

I thank my friends Joanne Vandenbrink and Nate Schultz for editing my book for me. Your time spent helping me is greatly appreciated.

I also thank my close friend Beth Putz for her continual encouragement to me in life, and in my writing.

A big thank you goes to my husband and friend, Greg who is my computer guru. Thanks for spending the many hours it took to get the book set up properly for publishing.

A thank you needs to go to my eldest son Tim who provided the cover photo. Tim, the Lord has given you quite a gift in photographing His creation. Tim's photos can be seen at https://www.facebook.com/thenarrowtwistyroad.

The biggest thank you goes to my Lord God who has given me the ideas and words to write this book. May this book draw people closer to you, and may You be given the honour and glory instead of me.

For by grace you have been saved through faith,
and that not of yourselves; it is the gift of God,
not of works, lest anyone should boast.
Ephesians 2:8-9

In Him we have redemption through His blood,
the forgiveness of sins, according to the riches of
His grace which He has made to abound towards
us in all wisdom and prudence.
Ephesians 1:7-8

FOREWORD

From Rags to Riches

When beginning to read a book, I appreciate it when the author gives some background about themselves. Most people without knowing me might assume, because this is a book about the Lord God, I would have a Christian background. When we buy a book with some sort of a biblical message, we figure and actually take for granted that the author is a believer in the Lord Jesus Christ. You may be surprised that my life today, and for the past thirty-three years has been radically different from my upbringing. Our childhood upbringing and experiences play a huge role as to who we are today. Even though I sometimes wish I had been blessed with a Christian family to nourish and guide me, I do believe the Lord had His hand on me all the way back. When the Lord in His mercy and grace takes someone and works in his or her heart, He uses even their past for good.

As a girl, people would probably have labelled me as a

happy go lucky kid even though I lived in a household where dissention was common. For some reason, even in trying times, I often seemed cheery and doing well. After attending a church Sunday school for two years and learning the fact that I was a sinner, who needed God to deliver me through Jesus Christ, I surrendered my life to Him. At the age of seven and living in a soon to be separated family, I was very attracted to the once a week lessons which taught of a Father who promised never to leave or forsake me. I still have the small Bible I won in those Sunday school classes for memorizing the most verses. Reading the Word of God daily didn't start until my later teens when I began dating my husband.

Being a young believer and living in a non-Christian environment, I lacked the support and encouragement to grow spiritually. I continued to attend the Sunday morning lessons, but was not encouraged to daily read the Bible which would have helped me immensely. Going to a secular high school was my testing ground, and I admit my downfall. Wanting to belong, I followed the crowd even when my conscience tended to bother me. By half way through my high school years, I had slowly slid into the world's ways of thinking, acting, and speaking. With my mom's second marriage not going much better than the first, family life was also tough. In those days I grew very thankful for my Christian grandmother and godmother. I saw my grandmother weekly and stayed at my grandparent's house often. She was an example to me in her prayers and godly lifestyle. My godparents visited often, and when my father left, we stayed at their house at least a few times a year. My godmother had no children of her own and took my brother and I under her wing. In high school, my godmother moved to England and then I wrote to her many times a year. She became my Christian mom and confidant. I had close fellowship with both and saw their walk with God as an example to me.

The years scurried by, and I grew into a young woman who would often be seen with a group of girls laughing and talking. I enjoyed school much more for the social contact than the education. It wasn't that I didn't like school, I did, but what I really looked forward to was the people. I wanted to be loved, so I often cared for and truly wanted to be a good friend to just about anyone around me. Even though I was part of one group of girls, I befriended many others. My closest friends were not the "in" girls, but I didn't mind. When I look back, this was just one small way the Lord kept me safe from a deeper life of sin. As our high school years were winding down, even my closest girlfriends and I were starting to experiment with the world's pleasures. By Grade twelve, I had participated in some drinking, tried pot, and was looking for trouble in my way of dress and desire for a boyfriend. Between my friends and I getting involved a little with all these things, I had lost most of my sense of right and wrong. This is where I believe I was headed in a dangerous direction.

At this point, the Lord intervened and showed me a better way by introducing someone into my life. On October 3rd, 1980, I met my husband to be at a Toronto roller skating rink. Not long after beginning to date, I realised that Greg was different; He didn't just believe the right things; he wanted his life to honour the Lord God and be a witness to others. From reading the Bible daily, he could actually talk about it too. Here I was a Christian, but not reading or growing at all in God's ways.

When we first started dating, I swore quite a bit. Does that shock you? As in many other aspects of my life, I was not following the Lord; actually didn't even seem to know how. One night Greg commented on my swearing, and so

I, not wanting to lose this guy, decided to pray that I could stop. I never swore again, amazing as it seems. It was the first of many prayers answered. On my seventeenth birthday, a little more than one month after meeting Greg, he presented me with a Bible. He suggested I read it daily. I also began to attend and soak in weekly Sunday sermons with Greg and his family. My life with Christ was changing, and I was too.

Those memories were from over thirty years ago, but are still important to see where I have come from. It has been quite the journey for me—one of learning and growing, repenting, and believing the Lord has a plan for me. The promises of God have and still do jump off the pages for me at times. I may have come from a very secular background, but the Lord continues to show me the rags in my life.

Do you have rags in your background, or even now? When I say rags, I mean the things in the past or present which you regret or realise were a problem before the face of God. It says in Isaiah 64:6 that all our good works are as filthy rags. Sometimes that can be hard to accept especially if you think you have led a fairly moral life. We were created to walk with God, have a relationship with Him and let Him lead our lives. If we are honest, we often desire to lead our own lives, go our own way, and not do what God wants. In the Bible, God says He desires our hearts and our lives to be lived for Him. His plan is to help us see and understand that if our heart is not His, bowed before Him and accepting of His will, then everything we do is filthy no matter how good the world and we ourselves think it is. That's not easy to accept, but true.

Thankfully, even though we are naturally selfish and sinful, God still has a plan for you and me. He desires a relationship with us and has made the way through His Son

Jesus Christ. When we believe and trust in God's Word and Spirit to guide us through this life, and into the next, He has good works planned beforehand for us to do (Ephesians 2:10). It is not me who does the good works; it is the Lord God working through me.

So, now you see how I really have gone from rags to riches. Maybe you wonder what riches are? Well, I would say riches are the blessings which result from a growing relationship with Jesus Christ through faith. They are the promises Christians can believe are theirs to hope in. Before my life with Christ, I lived solely for myself whereas now, I daily strive to live for my Lord and desire to please Him. I am not thinking, acting, and speaking in His ways to earn "brownie points", but because I am thankful for all He is, all He has done for me, and all He continues to do. This is not easy, and I am the first to admit, I stumble and fall every single day, and need to go to my Lord to forgive me again and again. I am rich, but not to the fullest yet. I still need my Saviour every step of the way. I have experienced so many of His blessings, but as this broken world continues to pull away from the Lord God, I yearn for the day when my faith shall be sight, when the Lord shall return for His people. Then like He promised, there will be no more pain, no more suffering, and no more sin (Revelations 22). Ah! Then I will truly see the riches of Christ to the fullest; then I will truly be home.

My hope and prayer as you read of my memories and learning through some very intense trials is that you too will begin to learn to yearn for the One who can give you true joy and strength even in the midst of this troublesome life.

O God, You are my God; early will I seek You;
My soul thirsts for You; My flesh longs for You
in a dry and thirsty land where there is no water.
So I have looked for You in the sanctuary, to see
Your power and Your glory.
Psalm 63:1-2

INTRODUCTION

From the very instant our lives begin, we are given the amazing opportunity to use our five senses letting us experience what life has to offer. I'm sure we all attest to our world being full of good food, wonderful scenes in creation, interesting information, and fun situations which can and do tantalize our senses. Whether rich or poor, strong or weak, we daily take notice of things which can be thoroughly enjoyed and definitely cause us to want more. Along with enjoyable experiences come times and situations which if we could, we would most certainly avoid. As we grow older, experiences take on a different perspective. In some ways, we actually begin to believe certain things to actually be our rights, even our deserved freedoms. We believe and begin to expect situations to go our way. This is our human nature or self-centered way of reacting to life.

Over the years, our ideas and beliefs take form and affect the rest of our lives. If we believe and trust in the Lord God as the Creator, we will seek to preserve life, and be thankful for the years we are given. Each day is a gift from God (James 1:17). Even when we know God is the giver of life, we still, in the back of our minds, tend to plan out how we hope our lives will go. However, if we read the word of God daily, we soon come to see how our thoughts may not be God's thoughts and our ways not His ways (Isaiah 55:8). This may bother or even disturb us sometimes, causing fear to rise up in our hearts. Our ideas and plans concerning our lives may not be the same as God's. This can be scary, but true.

As we age, people whom we care for, who may even be quite young, die or suffer a terrible accident. Not all people achieve the high age of eighty and are given the amazing blessing of great grandchildren. Some people aren't even given children, or the child they receive through a long sought after adoption turns out to be more of a problem than a blessing. If we focus too hard or too much on the situations which don't seem fair, or just not right, we take our eyes off of the great God who does have a good plan for each of His people.

The title of this book came to my mind at least two years ago and I know why. Over the past five years, our family has either heard of or been close to suffering, sickness and death in people who seem far too young to have to endure this. Five years ago in 2012, we came home from our summer holidays to be told some very sad news. The son of good friends of ours had died instantly in a bicycle accident. He was only eighteen. What a shock to us, and so very tragic! Then three and a half years ago, my husband's best friend, a very godly husband and father died of brain cancer in his mid-fifties. These difficult events were very hard to accept. Only three months after our friend passed away, other close family friends of ours experienced the awful nightmare of having their only son, just shy of sixteen drown at their family cottage. Adding to all these, shortly after this, a young woman friend to our three daughters passed away after a yearlong battle with an unknown illness. All these tragic events shook me to the core. I felt like my faith was being shaken. I couldn't even begin to imagine how our friends handled such hardships.

Little did we know what our own family would need to endure over the next two years. Our own eldest daughter was diagnosed with brain cancer in July of 2014. She fought a valiant battle and smiled almost right to the end trusting her Saviour to carry her home. Holly passed away in September of 2015. My worst nightmare had come true.

These trying and sometimes agonising times for our faith force us to either hang on to our beliefs with all our might, or toss them aside in utter discouragement. We choose either to reject God's thoughts and plan for our good even in this, or humbly accept that He knows best. Not easy at all.

My response to all of these situations of suffering has been a very slow, but steady growth of dependence on the Lord God. In reality, I had no one else to turn to. I wanted to be strong for my husband and children, but I knew that on my own, I was not able to go a step farther. One day about three weeks after our daughter's diagnosis, I found myself on my knees pleading with the Lord to carry me. As time moved on, I found the Lord teaching me ever so gently to trust Him like never before. I had to take His outstretched hand and let Him lead me through the valley of the shadow of death. When I gave myself to Him in absolute surrender, He was there. During the time of my daughter's illness, the Lord carried me when I couldn't even fathom how I would be able to go on.

The Lord has shown me how this earth is really not my eternal home. I used to fear many things, whereas now I am actually finding I am learning to leave my fears and heartaches where they belong. Interestingly, I seem much more at peace these days. I look forward to heaven much more now, where my Saviour is at the right hand of God. I also yearn for the new heaven and earth where my faith shall be sight, and where there will be no more sin, sickness, or sorrow. I am learning to yearn.

My hope with the writing of this book is to encourage you to lean on Christ. He is the only One who can teach you how to walk by faith and actually give you joy and peace even in the worst storms, while still in this sin-infested, sorrow-filled world. My prayer is that the Lord will use this book in some way to draw people away from focusing on their fears and stresses, and begin to learn to yearn for the Lord God. He promises that those who trust in Him will be given the strength to endure. May the Lord bless your reading of this book.

Notes

The Lord is my strength and my shield; My heart trusted in Him, and I am helped; therefore my heart greatly rejoices and with my song I will praise Him. The Lord is their strength, and He is the saving refuge of His anointed.

Psalm 28:7-8

1

What are you Yearning for?

Instead of giving a definition of the word yearning, I thought it might be easier to describe what yearning may look like. So, here goes. A feeling of yearning may be towards something, or someone, or it can be situational. It's when you find yourself wanting whatever it is intensely, or hoping for it prayerfully, and sometimes longing or craving it daily. These are a few quick ways that may aid us in understanding how yearning may manifest itself in our heart and our life. So, after reading them, what do you yearn for? Does this yearning or way of reacting tend to consume much of your time and thoughts? In reality, if we would honestly admit to it, we all yearn in one way or another at some point in our lives. Take a few seconds and think about the question again... what do you yearn for?

Maybe if I gave you some specific examples, it would help you better understand the concept of yearning. A quiet boy of twelve is sitting on his chair at his new desk. He has just moved into a busy neighbourhood and is adjusting to his new school. He knows absolutely no one in this city, but silently yearns for a friend. Every day at recess time, he attempts to hang around where the other preteen boys are playing. To him it appears no one wants to include him. As he walks home, he wishes silently that he could have at least one new friend. Time flies, and after a few weeks, the boy finds he is constantly wondering why he still has no friends to play with. He is beginning to think there is something wrong with him. His mother encourages her sensitive son to be patient, but his desire for a friend is all he can think of in his waking hours.

Another example is a woman in her late-twenties who has noticed that most of her peers are presently dating, engaged, or married. Some, even with eager expectation have begun their own little families. The get-togethers she once enjoyed have now all but disappeared. This woman secretly desires to be set in the same position; she would love to have a husband and family. It is hard to trust the Lord to provide in His timing and way. Day in, day out, month after month, she tries hard not to focus too much on this issue, but her thoughts often end up straying there.

One wife's thoughts often run to her hope to have children. This woman loves her husband very much and knows she is blessed to have one. As most women, she hopes to be graced soon with a family of her own. Sadly, so far it hasn't happened the way she and her husband had hoped. At church she weekly witnesses many of her fellow sisters seemingly "popping out babies" without any problems whatsoever. She tries hard to be happy for them and prays to trust the Lord with His plan for her. It is hard; how can she be content, or even push the yearning for a child out of her mind?

A middle-aged man used to be strong and able to do

almost anything he decided to tackle. Many people over the years had been encouraged by this man's caring and helpful ministering to them. Now, after a difficult doctor's appointment, he processes the tragic diagnosis of cancer. His whole life is changed in a flash; how will he be able to serve the Lord and others now? He knows and believes the Lord knows what is best, but how will that knowledge continue to satisfy his desire to work hard and serve others as the disease progresses?

Another man in his early fifties has worked at the same job for many years. He is thankful for his job, but never truly feels satisfied. The job pays the bills, but just barely. His tasks at work follow the same routine as they did ten years ago, and he's noticing he tires more easily now. If only he could find another job where he could make a difference in this world, and even feel comfortable to talk to others about his beliefs. He yearns to be used for good, and maybe even have the luxury of taking a holiday with his family once in a while without fear of going into debt.

Several more examples could be added, but I imagine you get the idea. Yearning is a part of life. We all yearn for something. The question remains what each of us truly yearns for, and why.

I believe it is in our human nature to yearn. God has put in each and every one of us a yearning for relationship. Many of the things we yearn or long for are right and good such as wanting a husband/wife, children, and friends to share with. It makes perfect sense that we want to keep in good health having the ability to work, serve, and even have desires for the people close to us to do well too. We all want to be healthy and happy in this lifetime. We all want to be useful on top of it all. There is nothing wrong with these yearnings.

Sadly, because of our self-centered, sinful nature, we may

also, above our natural yearnings, crave, and actually gravitate towards things or situations which are not helpful. This can be seen in wrong relationships and ungodly activities because of a yearning to belong or wanting what others possess. Coveting and greed are words we use more often when speaking of these particular yearnings. Even our habits of food, music, and the company we keep can and may eventually entice us to tread down dangerous paths, if we are not careful. Our times of yearning and our own selfish heart can and does many times lead us into unwanted and lifelong consequences. The Bible says in Jeremiah 17, that our heart is deceitful and desperately wicked. That means we often can't trust our own desires.

Why do we sometimes yearn for experiences which ultimately cause us pain? I believe we are seeking to fulfill what only God can. Everyone according to Romans 3 has fallen short of the glory of God. This means we don't measure up to God's standards; we actually can't measure up even if we tried our very best. Adam and Eve began life with a perfect relationship with God where they lacked nothing. When put to the ultimate test, they yearned for more, not realising they already had everything (see Genesis 3). They traded their relationship with God, and all it encompassed for the possibility of grabbing hold of a higher position. They believed Satan's lie, and separation from God resulted. Their life was now changed from one of precious perfection with God at the controls, to one of sin and self-centered ideas (read Genesis 1-3). When we pay attention to our yearnings, we will notice that whenever our yearning is not God's will, it will usually be short-lived lacking true happiness and peace.

God desires relationship with us; He wants us to love and seek Him above all else (Matthew 6). Did you know you were made by God, for God (Colossians 1:16)? Even though all was broken through Adam and Eve's sin and ours, God loved us so much that He sent His only Beloved Son Jesus Christ to die in our place for our sins (John 3:16). That's how much He loves us; He gave all for us, so we would see His sacrifice and yearn for an eternal relationship with Him.

Do you yearn for God? Be honest now. I know I have asked a hard question, but I believe an important one. If I had asked myself this question five years ago, I would have to honestly, but hesitantly say no, most of the time I did not yearn for God. Remember what yearning means. It means to crave or fervently long for something or someone. It wasn't that I didn't love God, or want a relationship with Him. It wasn't that I didn't want to know God more, or serve Him with my whole being. If someone mentioned looking forward to seeing the Lord face to face someday, or wishing the Lord would return right now, I would agree, but not with an intense yearning.

Over the past few years, the Lord began a new work in me. Sermons mentioned looking forward to the day when the Lord will return, and funerals talked about longing for the day we go to be with the Lord. I listened, but in truth didn't feel a real yearning to any great extent. It began to bother me a bit. I wondered if other Christians felt the same way. I looked forward to seeing the Lord face to face someday and to spend eternity with my Saviour, but secretly hoped that day might not come too fast. I wanted to see my seven children grow up, marry, and then enjoy the precious gift of grandchildren. I had to admit, there were many blessings I still enjoyed today right here in this world.

There was one thing I did begin to notice about Christians who seemed to yearn for the Lord's return, or the day when they would go to be in the Lord's presence.

They were in the midst of some sort of suffering or had been through much in their past.

A few years ago, my body started to show early signs of deterioration. Chronic health problems of various shapes and forms began to plague me, and sometimes limit my ability to serve. I'm not even that old yet, so this surprised me. I suddenly and sadly accepted I wasn't going to be able to accomplish some of the things in the ways I had assumed. At this point, I had been able to home school for many years, and was very thankful to make it almost to the end without these health problems getting in the way. My prayers at first focused on complete healing, but slowly over time changed to requesting help, strength, and contentment within the situation the Lord had allowed. I am human, so yes, I still prayed for healing. In Philippians 4:19, Paul tells us, "And my God shall supply all my needs according to His riches in glory through Christ Jesus. This became one of my favourite promises of God along with Philippians 4:13 which states "I can do all things through Christ who strengthens me." I began to depend on the Lord for His help more. He showed me these promises were true.

I noticed as time moved on, I would sometimes kid with my friends who were concerned about my health, about looking forward to my new body in heaven. I'd say with a chuckle that I wondered if maybe I could have it earlier rather than later. Do you yearn for the Lord to heal or release you from some infirmity or ongoing situation? I am slowly learning to trust more, and ask for the contentment needed to carry on in His way for me. It isn't easy to accept chronic problems, or any situation which changes our lifestyle. I admit, when times are hard, prayer comes more readily. Learning to yearn for the Lord's presence in stressful times often causes one to talk to Him more, and even begin to depend on Him. Even though I would rather not suffer the chronic problems, I am thankful for a closer prayer life with my Lord.

Do you go to the Lord with your difficulties and pains? Whether the trials are physical, mental, or spiritual, the Lord promises to be there for us and to guide us through. In Psalm 46: 1, it states, "God is our refuge, and Strength, an ever present help in times of need." Knowing God's promises from His word is a huge help and reminder for believers. To know those promises, you must read the Bible on a regular basis. Over time, you will notice that when you need the promise, it will be there in your heart and on your mind. This knowledge has comforted me greatly.

People say as we get older, we hear about or personally experience more deaths. At some point, the death of family, friends, and loved ones comes to all of us. If you read the newspaper, or listen to the news, death is a daily occurrence. Actually, death is a fact we all must face someday, and one we'd all like to skip if we could. Paul talks about death as the last enemy in 1 Corinthians 15. It is normal to want to avoid death and suffering. None of us wants to experience the death of loved ones. God has placed in us a desire to live, and death seems so very final. Our loved one is gone and it feels like we will never see them again. If you are a Christian, then you have the blessing of knowing the hope and anticipation of eternal life. If you love the Lord, and know you are lost without Him, then you will have a home in heaven someday. This should bring you peace (Isaiah 26:3). Thankfully the word of God encourages us with the fact that Christ has won the victory over death.

At the age of thirteen, my only grandmother passed away. Being very close to her made this quite traumatic for me. I knew she loved the Lord, so I would see her again someday, but heaven seemed so far away. Then over the following years, my parents also left this earth. When my step-father passed away, I experienced the first close person to me who died without having a relationship with the Lord Jesus. I struggled over his death. After a week of stressful grieving, I finally handed it over to the Lord. I had to believe He knew best.

With my husband being a family doctor, I sometimes hear about when his various patients are going through very trying circumstances, dying or have died. Some are very old, but some have been young. Over the years our family has been asked to pray for all ages of people. This has stirred in me a compassion for others who are suffering. I believe the storms in life come to all of us.

As I have mentioned, almost four years ago, my husband's best friend died of brain cancer. Now, this seemed far too close for comfort. As we watched him go through months of treatment, we witnessed the Lord helping and strengthening him and his dear family. I saw firsthand how the Lord draws his suffering servants closer to Himself, and how He guides them through the fiercest storms. The interesting thing I noticed was how our dear friends seemed at peace. As our friend drew closer to death he even seemed content and looking forward to heaven.

Secretly, I hoped our family would never have to go through some of these specifically heart-wrenching trials. Actually, to tell the truth, over the years I was often afraid of what God might allow into our lives. Suffering is not something people wish for, but will have to deal with in this broken world we live in. In the Bible it says, Christians shouldn't think it strange to have hardships and heartache throughout their lives (1Peter 4:12).

Suffering produces yearning. I believe suffering can make

Christians yearn more for God. When you suffer, do you go to God, or do you run from Him? What do you do when you are suffering?

Sometime in the last ten or more years I came to a general conclusion. In every difficult situation infiltrating our lives, we are either going to fight the Lord, or draw closer to Him. It doesn't help to fight; it actually makes it worse. We need the Lord, and it says in James that if we draw near to God, He will draw near to us. Situations that cause us to suffer greatly are not God working against us. Sometimes people get angry at God when storms in their life are raging. It is in our nature to feel the need to find someone to blame. Sometimes when tornados or earthquakes happen, people who don't even acknowledge God, blame him for the problems. We live in a broken world which manifests itself in many ways such as: illnesses, sinful behaviours and reactions, broken marriages, rebellious children, weather disasters, and much more. Many of the heartaches in this world are due to selfishness and our turning away from God. If we try to live apart from God, we can expect life in general to not go well (Gen.4).

So, let's get back to our topic. If we seek the Lord and His truth, then it should follow that when we suffer, we will naturally learn to yearn. God uses all situations for good for those who are called according to His purpose (Romans 8:28). What! You mean even terrible suffering? How is it possible when I suffer heartache and pain, that a good God can use it for the better? If you are a Christian, you might agree with the last few statements, even though it is tough to admit. We may not see the good right away, so don't worry. God's ways are not our ways, and God's thoughts are not our thoughts (Isaiah 55:8-9). Many verses in the Psalms remind us of how our God has much good in store for those who love Him. Dozens of other promises are full of hope for His people going through stressful trials. Read the Bible books Ephesians, James, and Colossians to find a whole bunch of them. Actually as we daily read the word of God, we will constantly find God's encouragements. Try to memorize even just a few and I'm sure the Lord will use them in your life. Because God's ways and thoughts are at times not at all what we would imagine, we also need to constantly ask Him to work trust in our hearts.

Here's the punch line: God never promised us a life of ease. Actually when you read the scriptures, it sounds like for a Christian who walks closely with his God, life is anything but easy. We are told to count the cost of being a Christian, and to expect hardship and persecution. This does not mean Christians do not experience blessings and wonderful things to thank the Lord for. Just stop for a second and ponder all of God's daily provisions and extras. In reality, God owes us nothing. In His grace, He gives us everything we need both spiritually and physically. In Matthew 6, God tells us not to worry; if we have food and drink, and clothing and shelter, we should be satisfied. In Ephesians 1: 3-4, it says that believers have been given every spiritual blessing. With those physical and spiritual needs taken care of, are you happy, and even yearning to learn more about this gracious God? An interesting comment I read from Max Lucado comes to mind; if the Lord only gave you salvation, could you be happy? Ponder that idea for a bit. I know it made me stop and think.

Now, we come to the crux of the matter. All those situations in life which we yearn for, and long to have, are they God honouring? If yes, then keep praying, but maybe change your prayer by ending it with these words, "If it is Your will Lord." I find this to be the toughest part.

Continue to pray for contentment to accept God's answer. If the answer is yes, then thank the Lord and ask for wisdom to use the answer for His glory. If the answer seems to be no, then ask the Lord for help to accept it and give you the will to move on to whatever He has in store. We need to believe His answer will "in God's eyes", work out for good. Sometimes God wants us to wait while depending on Him. Keep living for Him while anticipating whatever He will do in our lives. Be alert and often you will see the Lord work even amidst some of the worst scenarios possible.

Keep trusting, keep depending, and keep believing. All of us probably have some dream or wish that has never come to be. If we want something, we often want it quite specifically. This makes us less likely to see the blessings that can appear to satisfy the same desire but in other areas. For example, my godmother could not have children. She loved children, but the Lord said no. This must have been a terrible disappointment for her. She finally looked for work with young children. She ended up volunteering in a local hospital in the children's ward. Twenty-five years later, she received an award for her excellent work. In those years, my godmother also wrote a children's book for the sick children she loved so dearly.

I was also blessed by this same special woman during that time. My mother who was her best friend was going through two rough marriages. My mom visited my godmother a lot, and I became very close to my Aunty Joan. She became my "other" mother, my Christian mentor, and dear friend. I was very much like a daughter to her. Yes, my godmother didn't have the children in the way she expected, but she was fulfilled. God answered her request, just not the way she at first prayed.

Another example for trusting God comes from the time

when I was a little girl. I always looked for ways to pretend to be a teacher. As I journeyed through my school years, I noticed my marks indicated a lack in academics. Going to teacher's college demanded the necessary advanced marks which I did not possess. I sadly, but secretly told no one of my yearnings to teach. At the end of high school, I knew I had to decide what field of study to pursue. I had no idea except for the fact that I enjoyed children, art, and French. Most college courses required some experience in the field before entering. I proceeded to pray and look for a job with young children. I ended up working in daycares for the next six years. Here I enthusiastically decorated their walls with my drawings, taught songs and games to toddlers, and read many books. I was fulfilled in my job.

A few years later after much prayer, we decided to home school our children. I wondered how I would handle this huge responsibility. Remember, I didn't go to teacher's college. Surprisingly, this was where I thrived even though I did not have advanced academics or training. I became the teacher I had always wanted to be. Not my way, but God's way. Homeschooling was not by any means easy, but I was given the chance to put to good use, my joy and skills in art and French, and teaching in general.

Yearning for God is a learning process which encompasses our whole life. In good and bad times, the Bible encourages us through many of its writers to trust the Lord. Paul mentions in Philippians how he learned in all circumstances not be anxious over anything, and how to be content. He encourages us with the peace that passes all understanding which only comes through our Lord Jesus Christ. It is almost never an overnight change. Pray much, ask for wisdom, and believe that the Lord will teach you to yearn for Him. May the Lord help you to, "learn to yearn" for the only One who can truly satisfy your every desire.

Notes

Do not lay up for yourselves treasures on earth, where moth and rust destroy and where thieves break in and steal; but lay up for yourselves treasures in heaven, where neither moth nor rust destroys and where thieves do not break in and steal. For where your treasure is, there your heart will be also.

Matthew 6:19-21

2

Learning to Yearn for Eternal Things

It's time for tea. Yes, time for a short break with a hot cup of tea and the daily newspaper. I admit, I've never been one to read the paper from cover to cover, but mostly sort of browse and scan all the headlines, sales, weather, and obituaries. Each day for years, I would take this short bit of time in my afternoon to see what was happening in our part of the world. As time goes forward, our world continues to display its struggles and joys. Each day you can read about fights, murders, accusations, unpopular political decisions, greed, success, births, deaths, entertainment, and sports. Obviously, much turmoil is daily taking place on our planet, and it doesn't seem to be getting any better over time. Stress seems at an all-time high, while church attendance is falling to an all-time low. Things we never thought possible one century ago are now a constant, daily reality.

If you read the word of God on a regular basis, you will

not be at all surprised with the way our world is headed. The Lord warns us of a time when selfishness will reign and where the detestable will become acceptable (Romans 1). People need the Lord, but most have pushed Him out of their lives. Our society is becoming more anti-Christian all the time. Unfortunately, Christians in general have remained mostly mute when it comes to standing strong for what is right and good according to the Lord God. We have not only been quiet about certain subjects; we seem to have accepted the idea that there is nothing we can do to change the course of events. Maybe Christians think it is just too scary to let others know their positions on issues; they could lose their jobs, or their reputations. I must take blame here too, for I am sure there have been numerous times where I could have spoken up, or gotten involved somehow.

So what can we do? First, get into the Bible on a more regular basis. Second, start praying for our world and the events taking shape out there. Third, begin to recognise the times. We are living in dangerous, possibly end times, when our dependence on the Lord should be growing; we cannot afford to become despondent. In clinging to the Lord, we are promised we will gain strength and peace through these difficult times (Psalm 46). We need to learn to yearn for eternal things.

What are eternal things? Eternal means never ending or lasting forever. Only One is truly eternal; the Lord God of the universe. When we yearn for God, I believe we will begin to yearn for eternal things. The Lord promises heaven to those who believe His gospel through Jesus Christ. We will begin then to desire wholeheartedly to live for Him. Those people who are His children will be granted everlasting life; they possess hope for the future. When we seek those things which are above, we will look forward to that day. This present world is not the believer's final home (Hebrews 13:14). The Bible teaches us much about yearning for eternal things, or how we need to build up treasures in heaven. We cannot take our material possessions with us when we die, and the things we own cannot help us much when we suffer either. Yes, our earthly treasures may seem to be helpful to us in some respects, and even aid in our comfort in this sometimes, very trying life, but it's not enough. If we depend on material things to give us happiness in this life, we will be sadly disappointed. Only God can give true and lasting comfort and peace. But, where does true comfort and peace come from when the storms of life rage? How do we live through these years which seem spotted with terrible news and heartache?

So, what is eternal in this world? What or who can we trust that will truly last? As I have mentioned, the Lord God is the only One who has been and will be forevermore. If we have a relationship with Him through faith in Christ, we are instantly part of His eternal family. Then we can have comfort in life and in death. How will this cause me to yearn for eternal things? Well, if we love the Lord and His ways, then noticing the world daily straying further from Him should encourage us to yearn to be with Him. This should make us want to tell others of their need of Jesus. Also we will begin to long for this broken world to be free of sin. When we read the Bible and pray daily, we receive and feel His amazing presence and peace. Looking forward to Bible studies, church services, and fellowship with other believers is really the beginning of yearning for eternal things. Attending to these God-given teachings and comfort doesn't give us an escape to our problems, but begins to equip us to deal with them when they come.

Are you learning to yearn for eternal things yet? It's not easy, is it? This world entices us with so many of its dainties. We want what looks and feels good now, and when we have it, we want more-and as soon as possible, if you please. We have become very spoiled with such a vast variety of food, clothing, shelters, and entertainments. Most people have all their needs met, plus so much more. We have become so used to having everything at our fingertips that people in general are not longing for God. If we don't need God, then we won't even contemplate His awesome treasures in heaven either. Even believers can start to stray and forget about God, because we have so much.

I believe it is by the testing and trials of our faith which guide us into actually seeing our need for the Lord. In James 1, he talks about counting it all joy when you fall into various trials and hardships since the trying of your faith produces patience (James 1:3-4). Joy in hardship seems difficult to accept, but when it is perfected, makes us who God desires us to be. Hardships and trials can shape us into people of God.

Do we deserve a trouble free life? Shouldn't God just give us all a smooth-running life filled with nothing but amazing situations? We may think we would like this, but my guess is if we had a perfect life, we wouldn't very often need God, or so we might subconsciously conclude. If we didn't need God, we wouldn't seek Him, resulting in no real longing for eternal things. In my experience, we seem to learn to yearn for God and for eternal things when we are in need, suffer, or just aren't happy with our present day circumstances.

When it comes to what we deserve; the flat out answer is nothing except to be condemned, separated from God, and sent to hell, every single one of us. I know what I am saying seems so very harsh, but it says in the Bible, we are sinners who have fallen short of the glory of God (Romans 3:23). We haven't measured up and never will. But God, in His amazing love and mercy, sent His Son Jesus Christ to die for our sins, so we who believe could live eternally with Him (John 3:16). That's what grace means; undeserved love. In 1 John 4:8 it states, "We love God because He first loved us." We also read in Ephesians 1, that the Lord has given us believers every spiritual blessing we will need in this life. Knowing what God has so graciously done for us and given us should cause a strong resolve within to obey Him, and be content with our life. With the Lord in our life, we can trust He will be there for us providing what we need, when we need it. Paul in Philippians 3 and 4 speaks of "hands-on learning" in his life. He slowly found he learned through the many hardships how to be content in every situation. If you read about Paul's journey in Acts, his life was filled with stressful and life endangering predicaments. Paul speaks from experience. He learned that the Lord was there for him and would supply for His every need (Phil.4:19). Paul was learning to yearn for eternal things. Are you learning to yearn too?

How do I learn to yearn for eternal things? Pray for God to show you His eternal library of awesome wonders, and for a taste of what the new heavens and earth will be like someday. Seek to know the God who saved you. If you do not know Him, then start your search today. Ask the Lord to give you a thankful heart even amidst the trials that come. Pray for the ability to discern which things in this world are eternal and which are not. Pay attention and only go places where you know the Lord God would be pleased to find you there. Read books in which the Lord Himself would read. Focus on God honouring things (Philippians 4:8). Listen to and look at what would please our Lord. Everything we do, everywhere we go matters.

Eternal things are the things of God. Our world is full of objects and scenarios which seem ok, and don't seem really wrong to us at first glance. I wonder if we take the time and ponder a bit whether you too will notice many of them don't really aid us in our life with Christ now, or for eternity. Maybe prayer needs to be made more often for the decisions we make, even seemingly small ones. Learn to discern what is right and good in God's eyes. That's what's important, God's glory. In Psalm 119:37, the writer asks God to, "Turn away my eyes from looking at worthless things, and revive me in Your way." I'm sure it would be wise to add this little prayer into our lives.

Yearn to know Him who died for you, and what His will is while waiting for His return. Living in this world can be scary, but a lot less so with the knowledge that the Lord God is your refuge and help in troubled times (Psalm 46). Also, God encourages His followers with His Spirit, the Helper who will come, guide, and remind His children of what they need to know. Pray for His work in your life.

As you begin to strive to live a life pleasing to the Lord God, you will notice over time that your infatuation with worldly things begins to fall away. Your future is secure when you serve an eternal God. So, pray for growth in yearning for eternal things now. Then, oh then, His hope will fill your soul, and you will begin to sing, "Great is Thy Faithfulness! Great is Thy faithfulness! Morning by morning, new mercies I see; All I have needed, thy hand hath provided…Great is thy faithfulness, Lord unto me."

Notes

Finally, brethren, whatever things are true,
whatever things are noble, whatever things are
just, whatever things are pure, whatever things
are lovely, whatever things are of good report, if
there is anything praiseworthy—meditate on
these things.
Philippians 4:8

3

Learning to Savour the Moment

As we begin to yearn more for the Lord, He shows us things we might never have noticed before. As soon as the title for this chapter came to mind, a wonderful memory immediately followed.

One summer morning several years ago, while staying at a rented cottage, I decided to sneak out to the front deck to do my devotions. At this point in my life, it was a rare treat to have a few moments alone. This particular morning, as I tiptoed outside, my seven young children were actually still asleep. Sitting down and before opening my Bible, I glanced out across the still, serene lake only feet in front of the deck before me. Wow! I was immediately awestruck! The scene spread before me was absolutely gorgeous. Everything was completely still; even the birds weren't chirping yet. The smooth water and reflections from the picturesque lake immediately inspired me to worship our amazing Creator God. Before I thought about it, I was quietly praising Him out loud and thanking the Lord for showing Himself to me through His wondrous creation. My time in devotions that morning seemed deeper somehow, and I hated for it to end. I have never had a moment quite like that again, but it still remains a very special memory.

Do you have memories which you savour? I'm quite sure all of us have at least some extra good memories, memories that to this day continue to make us laugh or remind us of other good times in the past. In this busy world of ours, it sometimes feels as though we are constantly being rushed through life. Who has time today to think about events already past? We can get so caught up in our work, there seems less time to get together with others, which is often how many memories are made.

Something I've always enjoyed is family meals during which we reminisce about funny or memorable events from the past. This gets us all laughing and often even brings more stories to mind. I love to see my family joyfully savouring the moments we've experienced together. My children have called me, on occasion, a storyteller, and for the most part they are correct. I do enjoy seeing people smile and laugh while listening to one of my tales.

Do you savour the moments you are given? Do you remember each with a thankful heart? Do you wish you could repeat some of the extra-special ones again, but know in reality it was a once in a lifetime experience? As sinners, we are naturally selfish. This means we are self-centered, our focus and thoughts revolving around ourselves and what we want. As Christians, we are told to give thanks in everything (1 Thessalonians 5:18). Hopefully as Christians we gradually learn to be more and more thankful. Are you growing in thankfulness over time? Would your husband, children, friends, neighbours, and community say you are generally a thankful person?

The blessings we receive each day are abundantly spread out in front of us, and actually there are too many to even try to count. Have you ever stopped to ponder how many things we could be thankful for in just one day? Think about it. Did you sleep last night? Did you awake this morning? Did you sleep in a bed? Could you get out of bed and go to work to whatever occupation that might be? Did your car work when you headed out? If you don't have a car, do you have a way to go places, or can you walk? Did you find food to eat in your kitchen, and do you have a way to spend your time? Is the Word of God available to read in your house? These are just a very few of the basic things we are given by God daily. God's gifts are too numerous for us to even start to name them all. I only covered a tiny bit of the day to day blessings we enjoy and often take for granted.

What about extra blessings or events? Do you ever laugh, or thoroughly enjoy something? A few examples might be: a sumptuous meal, a fun get-together, an especially encouraging sermon or speech, a visit from a friend, victory over a hard temptation, safekeeping in a near accident, or maybe you could fill in the blank with something else. Do you remember those times and thank the Lord for them? I wonder if we paid more attention to the blessings God gives us and actually told Him, would we become more thankful over time? Savour the special moments God gives you.

Life is full of ups and downs. There are rotten days when pain, anxiety, and heartache tend to litter our way, but I hope we can also say that there are also good days when the sun shines, our day goes well, and we fall into bed that night happy for what took place. Certain events bring smiles to our faces; have we thanked the Lord for them?

In the Bible, there were ten lepers who approached Jesus.

Instead of recoiling and running in the opposite direction, Jesus did what was not expected; he held out His hand and healed them. Off they went, probably happy beyond belief, but only one happy and healed leper came back to say thanks. Are you like that one leper, or the ones who accepted the gift Jesus gave and left without a word? It's something to highlight in your thoughts.

I read a book awhile back called, A Thousand Gifts. The main idea I received from this book was to pay more attention to the amazing gifts God grants to us every moment of the day. It can change your life. I admit, I was somewhat surprised at the author's list which was quite different from what mine would hold, but that's ok. She thanked God for sparkling raindrops, moonlit nights, and many other things which most wouldn't even think to notice. Maybe it's time we did notice. Watch the birds make a nest, enjoy the breeze, and the cool nights and the quiet when the kids are all tucked safely in bed. Take an extra moment of time, it doesn't have to be much and savour the gifts of God. When you begin to savour what God has given, it can actually help with the rough stuff. Your focus will change.

There is always something to be thankful for. Maybe you think I sure must have an easy life to make such a bold statement. Well, I would say my life is easy in many respects, and harder in others. I grew up in an unhappy home which ended in divorce. The second marriage my mother entered was different but not really any better. Thankfully, I was blessed to be naturally cheerful even in tough times. I had lots of friends no matter where I lived. Even growing up in an unhappy non-Christian home, the Lord supplied for my needs. He gave me a Christian grandmother and godmother. He blessed me with a Sunday school bus which traveled down my street. I saw my need of the Saviour early in life. I am blessed to have a strong, Christian husband and several children. My husband has a good job, as do all of my kids. We live in a house and are all clothed well. We attend a strong, biblical church weekly, and all of our children show signs of having faith in our Lord Jesus Christ. I could go on and on with so many other blessings I am thankful for.

What about the hard things? My husband has a very stressful job that takes many of his waking hours. He also has diabetes which will someday take its toll. I have arthritis which often affects my hands, neck, and back. Chronic troubles with varicose veins in my legs are a going concern which can affect my activities at times. Our kids also have their various health issues.

As I have already mentioned, two summers ago our oldest daughter was diagnosed with brain cancer. That probably stopped you in your tracks. Yes, I said cancer, and she also had a husband and a very young son. Suddenly our life switched from struggling with the little health issues to one huge one. I was either going to sink or swim. I could either shake my fist at God, or kneel at His feet and ask for strength to go on. I knew it wouldn't help to ask why, so instead I asked what the Lord wanted me to do. I won't say I did fine all the time because that would be a lie. There were days, especially when each MRI test approached-and then after receiving the results that I struggled to see those moments God gives for us to enjoy. There were times I collapsed to my knees and told the Lord I could not carry the burden anymore. Thankfully, He graciously took it from me and granted His peace in return. Daily, I thanked Him for the strength to keep going. Daily I asked him to show me things for which to be thankful for, and He did.

We have to decide to be thankful even when a situation doesn't give us much strength or desire to do this. We can either wallow in our grief and sorrow, or we can depend on the Lord for what we need. He will supply; He promises (Phil.4:19, Psalm 34:19). So many promises in the word of God lead us to humble ourselves, to acknowledge our weakness and trust Him who is the only One who can and will lift us up (James 1).

The Lord has provided. Our daughter and son in law strived to stay focused on the Lord. Throughout the time of our daughter's illness they were constantly being a witness of His goodness. It was not an easy time with all the many appointments, tests, treatments, and much waiting. My daughter amazingly continued to smile all the way through, until she physically couldn't anymore. She was a picture of a woman who trusted her Lord even in the very worst of times. Her first comment to me after hearing she had a brain tumour was that "God doesn't make mistakes." During the next year, Holly smiled, laughed, joked, and continued to trust Him. She believed that even in this the Lord would work things out for good. My daughter walked throughout town with her son in the stroller and people noticed how well she looked, and how happy she appeared. We found much to be thankful for even amidst the diagnosis of cancer. My precious daughter went to be with her Lord and Savour fourteen months after the first MRI. I am forever thankful for the time we were given. I spent more time with Holly and her son in those last months than ever before. I learned to savour and cherish the memories.

We can dwell on the negative or focus on the blessings. I miss Holly greatly, and there is a definite void in my life now. Our family will never quite be the same, but that doesn't have to mean the end to times of thankfulness and joy. Look for them, savour each one now, because life is short and time is precious. You may not have tomorrow, so remember each day is a gift given to you from God. What are you going to do with the time God has graced you with? Are you going to focus on the storms, or will you join me in striving to be more thankful to the Lord? Ask Him to help you grow in being thankful even amidst this broken world. I know He will.

The Lord never promised us an easy life, but He has promised us His strength, peace, and guiding hand as we go through the trials. I can see how the Lord is carrying this out in my life. The Lord has proven to me over and over how His promises are true and real, and for every child of God to claim. At times I need to be carried, other times I feel Him right beside me encouraging me to keep on going. Trust Him, depend on Him, and He will help you as you go through even the toughest of predicaments. If you look for them, He will give you things to be thankful for, even in the bleakest moments.

God never promised you or me, or anyone on this earth that they would live to be ninety years old, or that we would all be healthy and strong, or marry and have children. I think we all assume we will do just that. We live and act like we expect God to give us everything our heart yearns for: a long and happy marriage, compliant and healthy children, new house, reliable cars, extra money, holidays, and a retirement where we can relax and travel in our healthy, old age. When even just one of these doesn't work out, if we are honest, we tend to feel cheated. If we pay attention, we might start to see how gracious God really is.

Take the time and start savouring each moment. It might just change your whole perspective on life. Oh, and remember to thank God when you notice the innumerable blessings He has placed right in your own space. He is gracious. Learn to savour the moments God gives.

The Lord's Prayer

Our Father, who art in heaven, hallowed be
Your name, Your kingdom come, Your will be
done, on earth as it is In heaven, Give us this
day, our daily bread, and forgive us our debts, as
we forgive our debtors, and do not lead us into
temptation, but deliver us from the evil one, for
Yours is the kingdom, the power, and the glory,
forever. Amen.
Matthew 6:9-13

4

Learning He is not Santa Claus

As I have mentioned earlier in the book, I grew up in a
basically non-Christian home. Christmastime was all about
watching the annual shows like Rudolph the Red Nosed
Reindeer, Frosty the Snow Man, and looking forward to
receiving what you asked for from Santa. At the age of
seven, I came to a point where the weekly Sunday school
lessons were beginning to sink in. I now understood the
fact that I was a sinner and that Jesus Christ had come to
this earth to die in my place. Because of Christ's sacrifice
for me, I could be forgiven and go to heaven someday.
Soon after coming to these conclusions, the Lord opened
my heart to accept Him as my Saviour and King.

So, how does this beginning lead us into the topic of
Santa Claus, you say? Well, every Christmas season after
the Lord worked in my heart turned into an experience of
spiritual growth for me. Even though I still thoroughly
enjoyed and looked forward to giving and receiving gifts on

Christmas Day, I also now knew the real reason for the day was Christ Jesus' coming to this earth to live and die in our place. Every Christmas night, after finally going to bed, this fact would suddenly resound in my head. Next, guilt would creep into my thoughts as I acknowledged that I had not even thought about Jesus all day until then. Following this, I prayed and admitted my neglect of my Lord, while proceeding to thank Him for the best gift.

In case you aren't familiar with North American Christmas traditions, here are a few facts to bring you up to speed. Santa Claus is an old and plump, white-bearded man who is decked out in a red suit. Parents line up in malls in the month of December, so their child will have their chance to sit on Santa's lap. Santa smiles and laughs, and promises to bring each child all the presents they so desire. Apparently if you are well behaved, you are sure to receive them. It's also said that if you write a letter to this jolly old elf, he responds by delivering your desired presents right to your tree on Christmas Eve. The tradition states this takes place Christmas Eve after the children are nicely snuggled in bed. Oh, and don't forget to leave out the cookies and milk for Santa and his reindeer. In high school I had a girlfriend whose father would actually climb up on their roof soon after the kids went to bed, so they would believe Santa was arriving with their gifts.

Perhaps, I was one of those children who believed in Santa, until about the age of eight. On Christmas Eve, Mom would tell us we simply had to go to sleep, or Santa might not come. I usually took a very long time to fall asleep because of all the excitement. One very late Christmas Eve, while lying on my bed awake, but with eyes closed, I heard someone creep quietly into my room. Excitedly, I figured it must be Santa. I then opened my eyes just a crack to take a peek at the visitor, and to my disappointment saw it was my own mother quietly placing my brother's and my stockings on the end of our beds. So, I thought sadly to myself, Santa was not really the gift giver I had been taught. It had been my mom all along.

As a child with a selfish nature, it didn't take me too long to get over my disappointment and continue to be happy when I still got most, if not all of what I asked for each year. But what about when you don't get what you want in life? Do we continue to be thankful for what we do have? As we mature, we come to accept the truth that we do not always receive everything we ask for in life. I do remember one Christmas when I desperately wanted the new doll who could actually walk. I'd seen the ads on TV and was totally hooked. However, I didn't end up receiving the walking doll, and probably pouted dramatically when coming to the end of the unwrapping with no appearance of the coveted item.

So, if God is not like Santa Claus, how should we pray to the Lord? When we converse with the Lord, it is understandable our prayers often take the form of asking for this and that. Some requests are good and right, "Lord, help me to have wisdom and be a witness at my work", or "Lord, our congregation is in need of a minister, please provide for us soon." Even requests for the Lord to take a hard trial away, or heal a sickness are fine. The Lord knows our heart, and He tells us to come to Him when we are burdened, and He will promises to give us rest (Matthew 11:28). Do you take your burdens to the Lord?

Many of us grew up at least hearing about the ACTS method of how to pray which consists of: Adoration, Confession, Thanksgiving, and Supplication. Or what about the Lord's Prayer, which is a little more specific? Do we pray this way, or are you like me and must confess, most of our prayer life falls into asking for things, and telling the Lord how you want events to go? We might even add to the end of our prayers at times, "if it is Your will Lord", but again, if His will is totally opposite to ours, how easily do we accept it?

How do we pray to the Lord God? I would imagine examples would be numerous of the various types of prayers each of us prays. Do you praise and respect the Lord God when approaching Him in your prayers? Do you lift praise up to Him for who He is when you approach His throne of grace? Our society seems to in many ways have lost its respect towards God and our fellow man. Even Christians can become so familiar with the Lord that over time could result in a loss of the respect and honour due to Him. Just the fact we are given the privilege to be able to pray to the Lord is a gift of grace. It is only because of Jesus's death that we can through faith have access to the throne room of God. Remember to thank the Lord for this grace.

Do we see the need to confess our sins and faults to the Lord on a regular basis? If we figure we don't sin every single day in some way, then we had better re-examine our hearts (1 John 1). The Lord God promises, "If we confess our sins, He is faithful and just to forgive us our sins, and cleanse us from all unrighteousness (1 John 1:9). If the Lord is so merciful and gracious, shouldn't we want a tender heart to see and confess our sins? Ask Him to teach you how to hate your sins, to turn in repentance, and then turn away from the sin, and do what is right.

Does thankfulness regularly overflow into your prayer life, or are you often complaining to Him for the way life is treating you? We do live in a broken world, and in broken bodies. I don't believe God ever originally intended us to be sick, suffering, or sad, but it is through our disobedient nature these things have come to be. We can't even blame our first parents Adam and Eve who were the first to sin, because we commit our own sins every day. When we read the word of God regularly, and meditate upon it, I believe we will come to be more thankful for His amazing grace and mercy which He bestows upon us every single day of our lives.

Lastly, if we were to follow the ACTS' method of praying, supplication would be last. Supplication means the things we ask of the Lord. What do your supplications include? Do you humbly ask for daily wisdom, contentment, patience, and energy to do whatever He desires us to do, or are your prayers filled with how you want circumstances to go in your life? I imagine we all could use some growth in this area.

So, what can we do to change our prayers in such a way so God is lifted up, praised and honoured? Jesus is our example; He treated God His Father in a revered, respectful, honouring, and adoring way. Jesus walked and talked with God as He journeyed through every circumstance. He talked about others to God the Father in a caring way; He desired God's best for them (John 17). When He prayed to God the Father, He prayed for help, yes, but also thanked God and asked for His will to be done.

When we pray for our loved ones, do we ask the Lord to help us love them, no matter how they treat us? Do you pray that God's will be carried out in their lives? Jesus had a ministry of caring and sharing. Do we pray for help to live as ambassadors of God's love to others? God knows our heart, but He wants us to love each other His way. Pray for His hand to guide you to love like Jesus. When we change our prayers from only thinking of ourselves to what God wants, circumstances with others may begin to change for the good.

Are we content when things don't go as smoothly as we'd hoped? How did Jesus react when situations changed seemingly mid-stride? Well, He usually prayed, and drew close to the Father. More than once He was heading off to pray or rest, and then the crowd or sick ones were right there pleading for His immediate attention again. Did He send them away? No, He handled the situations as they came. Paul talks in Philippians about learning to be content. As we put our trust in the Lord, we should continue to strive to do what is right in His eyes. He will provide the wisdom and contentment you need to press on.

God does not always give us what we want. Sometimes not getting what we hoped for is a struggle especially when it comes to our health, relationships, jobs, or just every day encouragement. One fact we should try to remember is that God knows what is best for each one of us. His plan is good, even if it takes us through many rocky, thorny hills and dark valleys to get there. In Psalm 23, the Lord is my Shepherd, I shall not want......He promises I will not lack anything He feels I need. He promises to be my shepherd who will lead and guide me. He will do what is necessary to take me through the valleys where it feels like I am totally lost. The Lord also promises a future to those who believe and trust in Him. When you read His word daily, He assures us of His constant presence in a world of chaos and uncertainty. Between the lines of many of God's promises are the words, "Trust me."

When God seems to say no, ask Him to help you respond with a calm and firm assurance of His presence as you walk on. In one of my favourite Psalms (34), the Lord has shown me quite a few times how when the righteous cry out to Him, He delivers them. Does that mean my troubles will disappear, or that my wants will be heard and given? Maybe not, but if we trust His ways, and His plan, then whatever the outcome, it will work for our good. Strong believers in Christ will often bear witness of how Christ felt the closest when they were in their deepest, darkest moments. These were the times when they were led to pray more and maybe even unexpectedly grew spiritually. They learned to trust and depend more, and believe what God says to be true. I admit, I still hate suffering and those heart wrenching trials. I would like life much better if I could just grow spiritually without them. However, the Lord has taught me much through the hard knocks of life. Some of the verses I've come to treasure over the years are all to do with trusting, and receiving His peace to endure. God will carry His people through the storms, and continue to work in their hurting hearts as they trust His good plan for them. We need to trust Him, as He leads us through the dark valleys.

You see, Jesus is not at all like Santa Claus. Jesus gives the best things to those who believe and trust in Him. He grants us what we need to survive in this broken world and actually be at peace. He teaches and prepares us for an eternity in heaven. In Matthew 6, Jesus reminds the people to seek His kingdom first, and He will make sure our needs are taken care of. Remember, this is not our eternal home (Hebrews 13:14). Only God knows what each one of us needs. Now, I ask you, after reading this chapter, do you think your prayers to the Lord God will change? Lean on Him, trust His path, and accept the strength He offers as you make your way through this sometimes difficult, trial-filled life. He really is the giver of abundant life if we'd only take our focus off of the things we can't have, and take the necessary time to see and enjoy the benefits of having the good Shepherd guide us through this life, and into glory. Pray to the Almighty provider who is real, and waiting for you to lean on Him. Have faith Jesus will give us what we need to live in this life, but keep in mind, He is not at all like Santa Claus.

Notes

Notes

And my God shall supply all your needs
according to His riches in glory by Christ Jesus.
Philippians 4:19

5

Learning to Relax Your Grip

Many years ago, while in my early twenties, I learned how to crochet. Believe it or not, my husband was the one who taught me. His grandmother had taught him this craft when he helped for a few summers on their farm. We still have the red, white, and blue Afghan he made somewhere in our home. I myself did complete a few what I felt were pretty primitive looking Afghans that definitely were not, in my opinion, anywhere near perfect.

From there I decided to move on to something I had always wanted to make-a crocheted doily. Much more effort was needed while stitching these delicate pieces. They required specific and careful attention to each instruction. With no one to example this fine craft to me, off I bravely ventured crocheting my first doily. After stitching quite a few rows, I noticed a problem beginning to surface. It was obvious I had stitched the beginning rows too tight. I tried again, but not far into it, discovered the same concerning look to the stitches. The bump rising through the middle of my finished parts was easy to spot. This was frustrating; Maybe, I pondered, I should quit while I'm not too far into it. I remember showing my husband and listening to his advice to try relaxing my grip on the thread, making the stitches looser, resulting in a flatter doily. I sighed, and began again, working hard at not stitching so tight. This time my crocheted piece turned out much better. Many doilies followed over the next years, but if I am honest, I think they were still a bit too tight.

Releasing or relaxing your grip is not a simple endeavour, especially if you don't realise what you're doing. I assumed at first my crocheting was going along just fine, but the end result proved me wrong. Do you hold on too tight to things? Here's another example of holding on too tightly....when I first started driving, my hands would often end up going all tingly after a short period of time. Why? Well, I was nervous, so as a result, I held onto the steering wheel rather tightly. When I paid attention, or was reminded, and released my grip somewhat, I found I actually relaxed and enjoyed the drive more. I still find I tighten my grip when driving in dense fog, or a snowstorm.

Do you find yourself holding on to anything too tightly? Think about it for a minute. How about your family, especially your spouse, children, or even your parents? Do you need to be reminded to release your grip? Has your holding too tightly caused other issues to surface over time? Maybe this is a totally foreign idea to you. As we learn to yearn for the Lord Jesus Christ and His truth, we also come to the place where we need to let go, or relax our grip in other aspects of life. We need to let God take control. We need to trust Him.

Let me lead you to meditating a little deeper into this topic. Children are a gift from God (Psalm 127). We are privileged to even have them. Most parents would admit that there are stages and fearful situations when they wanted to hold on extra tight to their precious little ones. In fearful scenarios, this is totally understandable. We love them so much, and we see all the potential dangers which could occur. However, if we overprotect or control our teenagers, it may result in them wanting to get away from our uncomfortable grip. I'm sure this is not what we intend at all.

There may be other times when we hold on too tightly, such as our positions or jobs, our health, the past, money, pride, and even our freedoms. Maybe you can think of other examples where we may find ourselves holding on too tightly. I don't think we necessarily hold too tight on purpose, like my crocheting and my driving. We need to remember, it is the final outcome that matters.

Someone told me once that our children are lent to us by God, and we would do well to remember that they ultimately belong to Him. While on this earth though, we do have a tremendous responsibility to take care of the family we are given. Most would agree we bring them up so they can function as normal human beings out in society and hopefully, develop a strong desire to serve the Lord God. If our actions and words speak of fear much of the time, how will it affect our family? As I write this, I am saddened because I know my fears over the years have probably in some way affected my children. I am thankful for the promise of forgiveness and the help given to move on and learn to react in God-honouring ways. God is so gracious and merciful; He forgives and uses even my past failures for good. He has shown me, the path to walk, and hopefully I can in some way, bear witness of what I have learned.

If we are Christians, we know we should trust the Lord.

He wants us to place our life in His hands. God's promises are sufficient to give us what we need to relax and trust everything to His control (Matthew 6, Philippians 4:4-8). I don't know about you, but I have never done well at leaving my requests totally with the Lord. It's like I'd pray, and then upon saying Amen, I'd stick the concerns back into my pocket.

To what else do we tend to hold on too tightly? In my reading of the Bible, God instructs us to trust Him with all of our heart, and lean not on our own understanding, in all our ways, to acknowledge Him, and He will direct our path (Proverbs 3:5-6). Another verse says to deny our self and take up our cross and follow Jesus (Matthew 16:24). In other words, we are to take our hands off of the things which we cannot control, and place our lives in God's hands. He knows better than anyone what we need, and can be fully trusted to lead us where He knows we should go. Sounds easy, but for most of us, it is terrifying to take that leap of faith and learn to trust and not fear. God knows. I read a short piece one evening about a woman who stated that she had looked up "Fear" on Google. It said there are three hundred and sixty-five verses with encouragement "not to fear" in the Holy Bible. That's encouragement for each day of the year. We surely need that, and God has provided. One of the verses I've memorized years ago on the topic of fear has stuck in my mind, and it's short. "Do not be afraid, only believe" (Luke 8:50b, Mark 5:36b). Another one I try to keep close to my heart is, "When I am afraid, I will trust in You" (Psalm 56:3).

We like to be in control, but unfortunately, when we try to steer things the way our hearts direct, the situations do not usually work out, especially if we react in haste. Sadly, if our emotions try to deal with difficult people or scenarios, and it doesn't go the way we hoped, we tend to hold on even tighter. For instance, if we never let our children fall or make mistakes, and be willing to leave them in the Lord's hands, what example is shown of trusting our God who promises to lead them?

Some other examples of not trusting might be....what if you are having a difficult time dealing with a lazy person at your work, and instead of praying and waiting for the Lord to show you how to react, you blow up. Instead of your boss noticing the issue with the other person, he now sees you as the one having a problem. Maybe the reason you blew up was because you were holding tight to your work position and didn't want this co-worker to make you look bad. Another example could be if your children are starting to listen to types of music you deem as ungodly and not beneficial for them. Instead of praying and asking for wisdom, you start yelling at them to turn off that garbage. If you had given the concern to the Lord, maybe He would have shown you how to gently explain to them why you believe the music was offensive to you and the Lord.

Part of the issue might be the fear of not having any control. The Lord knows our anxieties, and He cares much more than we could ever imagine. He wants us to come to Him and lay our burden down. Tell him what is happening, and how we are feeling. I know it is a difficult thing to do, but we need to learn to let our hold on our fears go. We need to pray for wisdom and strength to trust that the Lord will be true to His word and work the difficult things out. Ask Him to show you how to react, and what to do and say no matter what happens. The Lord promises blessing to those who commit their way to Him.

Some of the issue may be our unwillingness to change and grow. I believe sometimes God allows hard trials, so we will learn to depend on Him more. I know my experiences would say this is true. Maybe you have noticed how hardships, sometimes gut wrenching tragedies happen to seemingly good people, Christian people. God wants us to strive to use these trying times for His glory. Paul in the book of 2 Corinthians says that, "We are hard pressed on every side, but not crushed; we are perplexed, but not in despair; persecuted, but not forsaken; struck down, but not destroyed..." With Christ carrying us, and giving us strength, we can bear witness of His amazing peace during the storms of life. "Therefore, we do not lose heart. Even though our outward man is perishing, yet the inward man is being renewed day by day. For our light affliction, which is but for a moment, is working for us a far more exceeding and eternal weight of glory" (2Corinthians 4:16-17).

For some strange reason, we still subconsciously may decide we can achieve the best changes and results if we tackle the concerns on our own. We lean towards being so very proud in many ways. In truth, who do we think we are....God? Only God sees all, knows all, and can direct us in the best way to go. Yes, it is an act of faith to let our tight grip go. It is also an act of faith to go through life with hands open surrendering to His plan, instead of tense, white-knuckle gripping. Daily we need to ask for help to give our concerns, fears, and hardships into His capable hands. This could be what the Lord God means when he instructs us to pray unceasingly (1 Thessalonians 5:17). Take it to the Lord in prayer, and cast your burdens upon Him, for He cares for you (1 Peter 5:7). My experience of praying lots throughout my day is that the Lord's peace resides in me quicker, and my mind doesn't do the "what ifs" as much.

So, if you are honest, and look at your life, do you see where maybe you need to begin to release your grip? Start by listing all the things you possess in your care such as:

money, time, family, friends, church, home, school, jobs, community, books, music, toys, energy, health, food, clothing, cars, and anything else which is part of your life. What is important to you right now? Is it your position at work? Do you fret over the issues taking place there? Maybe it's time your tense grip on it was released, and you begin to trust in the Lord's control over all things.

So, are you placing your trust in the Lord? How about your finances? Are you constantly worried you might not get that promotion, or what if you are the next one to be let go? At church, maybe you are the president of a committee. Do you take each meeting, each decision to the Lord first, or do you fret and maybe even complain about the issues to your friends and family when things aren't going well? I've failed in these things too, so you are not alone. I already mentioned husband, and especially children, but these are probably areas where our trust can be relatively small, and our fears awful big. We are instructed in the Bible to take everything to the Lord in prayer (Philippians 4:6-7). Nicely, there is a promise at the end of verse 8 saying when we give it over, the Lord will grant us His peace. Strive to go to Him first with every struggle, and it will make a world of difference in your life physically, mentally, and spiritually.

We plan out our lives, don't we? When we have children, we tend to automatically assume that we will be the ones bringing them up, then sending them off to college, where they will end up getting a job, marry, and then give you many precious grandchildren. Oh, and don't forget the hope someday far into the future, that your children will take care of you when you no longer can do it yourself. No wonder we are devastated when some part of the plan doesn't go the way we presumed. An illness, accident, disease, or just one big, unexpected event takes place. You get sick, lose your job, or get in an accident which changes the course of your whole life. What if the longed for desire to travel the world just isn't going to happen now. Maybe the job you always wanted is taken by someone else. Maybe you didn't end up married, and have the children like you hoped.

What is our natural reaction, when we don't receive all we desire or think we deserve? Often our reactions can be somewhat selfish and demanding. We can get angry and sometimes increase our grip. We become defensive about our words and actions, even if deep inside we know it is wrong. God wants us to seek Him and His kingdom first, and then He promises to bless us with what He knows is best for us (Matt.6). Sometimes I wish I possessed a mind which instantly brought up the Word of God instructing me in every situation. I yearn to physically see the Lord by my side, and have Him tell me how to handle every issue which arises. Sadly, I must not really have thoughts like this enough, or I would be praying nonstop to keep the awareness of the Lord's presence with me. He is there, I know, but it is difficult to constantly make the decision to let my time on this earth be given into His hands. I worry. What will happen if I truly let God have control over my life? What if He allows something I deem as over the top?

Well, as you have read in another chapter of this book, something very difficult has happened in our family's life. My dear daughter died at the age of twenty-six. If that isn't the toughest thing to happen in my life so far, then I don't know what is. I used to hear about these awful hardships happening to others, so it shouldn't have been that big of a surprise when we too suffered. None of us are immune to suffering or huge trials. In truth, I must admit, I hoped silently that those agonising heartaches would never hit our family. For years I used to wonder when the bomb was going to strike us, especially when we'd be praying for the trials of others. I would even every once in a while when our various friends were suffering, express this fear to my husband and close friends. Calling the trials a bomb was not a very proper way to put it, but it is the truth. I was deathly afraid of what God might allow into our lives.

Tension and fear tend to cause physical changes to take place within our bodies. Some get stomach aches, some bite their nails, make unreasonable comments or become angry people. The tension of my daughter's cancer coupled with accepting I had no control caused me thankfully to pray more. I began to see the desperate need of handing my fears over to the only One who could give me true peace and security. Don't get me wrong, I still have a strong tendency to be anxious or stress, and because of it, have chronic neck strain which is the painful reminder I receive indicating my lack of trust. I have been very slow to learn to depend on the Lord to lead and guide me through the tough stuff in life. I can say, I am learning to relax my grip, but still have a long way to go.

We live in a broken world because of sin, and because of this brokenness, our world and bodies are damaged. It is actually an amazing sign of God's grace that we are as healthy and happy as we are. It is amazing that there are not more hurting people and situations because of sin and how everything has been affected by it. God is not at fault when disasters happen, or when our bodies don't work right anymore. However, remember, God does promise to work good through those situations for those who love Him (Romans 8:28). I can believe this even though my dear daughter died. She suffered from a broken body unto death, but her memory to all who knew her holds such a witness of our Lord's workings in her short time on earth. Holly left this earth with a confidence in her Lord's promise of eternal life to those who love Him. She trusted that her God was in control. I must also believe this truth of God. Do you believe God will work good in your life? Do you love God? If you do, then you can believe this promise too.

So, how can we live in a broken world and somehow release our grip of control? I can only speak from my own experience. When a situation is on my mind a lot, and I come to see that I am stewing over something that's happened, or going to happen, I now go to my room and kneel down. God says in James, "Humble yourself in the sight of the Lord, and He will lift you up." Tell the Lord the issue at hand, pour out your fears and difficulties, and then ask Him to take them from you, and replace them with His amazing peace and strength. He promises to help us. I am learning to leave my trials in God's hands more, and seem less tense after praying for help. We need more prayer, and less holding on to the controls we never really had in the first place. Psalm 23 reminds me of the importance of remembering that I am a sheep and the Lord is my Shepherd. Read it for yourself again, and drink in His care and guiding hand. He wants the best for His beloved sheep.

The Lord is my shepherd, I shall not lack anything, He makes me to lie down in green pastures, He leads me beside still waters, He restores my soul, He leads me in the paths of righteousness for His names sake. Yea, though I walk through the valley of the shadow of death, I will fear no evil, for You are with me. Your rod and staff they comfort me. You prepare a table before me in the presence of my enemies; You anoint my head with oil; my cup runs over. Surely goodness and mercy shall follow me all the days of my life; and I will dwell in the house of the Lord forever.

God knows what is happening in your life, yesterday, today, and for the rest of your life. Give your situations to Him; release your grip, and expect the Lord to work. His amazing peace is beyond our comprehension, and His strength above amazing. Trust Him, and learn to yearn that His control and plan be what you desire and accept. Let your fear turn to faith by resting in His care. He won't let you down.

Notes

Trust in the Lord with all of your heart, and lean
not on your own understanding; In all your ways,
acknowledge Him, and He will direct your path.
Proverbs 3:5-6

6

Learning to Be Led Step by Step

When this title came to me, a memory to start it off instantly followed. The timing was about one week before my dear daughter Holly passed away from brain cancer. I had been over at her house that evening which is only a quick two minute drive. The realization my daughter was going to die, and soon, hit me hard that particular night. Some might say, "Didn't you have lots of hints of this coming?" Yes and no. Death is a shock to everyone, no matter the timing. When my daughter was still doing well for the many months after diagnosis, and even after going through radiation and chemo, I found myself relaxing and enjoying our times together. After hearing the cancer was back, everything began to change so very quickly. Now it became more and more obvious that no intervention was going to stop this terrible enemy's pursuit. I still believed God could heal her if it was His will, but knew deep in my heart there was a very good chance she would leave us.

That evening, my husband and I had come to the house separately. So upon leaving, we each traveled alone those couple of short minutes back to our home. As I slowly made my way to the car, hating to leave Holly and Jeff, I felt so very burdened, weak, and sad. After starting the car, and leaving the curb, the next song on the CD began to play. It was a song by Steven Curtis Chapman. If anyone doesn't know him, he and his wife have also been through a very difficult death of a dear daughter. Anyway, the chorus began to play, and I heard, "Take another step, take another step, when the road ahead is dark, and you don't know where to go, Take another step, take another step, Trust God, and take another step." I Googled it to give you the exact words, and the whole song is so beautiful, so applicable. Anyway, through my tears that night, while pulling into our driveway, I had to smile; God knows, and He provides. I thanked the Lord right there and then for His care, and asked for the needed strength to carry on through this fierce storm.

Do you feel like you are in a storm that just isn't going away? I went to a speech recently and the speaker made some interesting comments which remain with me today. She said we are all either heading into a storm, already in the midst, or coming out of a storm. Storms tend to come in all shapes and sizes, but everyone must go through them. Storms are the difficult circumstances we all encounter some time in our lives. They burden us and tend to drag us down. Storms often take our focus off of God and onto the issue at hand. The woman who spoke at that Ladies Day had gone through the storm of having her eighteen year old son die of cancer.

The important question remains, "What are doing in your storms?" How are you faring? Are you crying out to the only One who can and does provide the necessary and helpful tools you need to ride through it? Or are you trying to trudge through the mud and debris on your own strength?

Another question, are you learning anything in this storm? God wants us to learn to depend on Him every step of the way. Yes, one step at a time, with Him right there helping you through. There is no way I could have gone through the death of my daughter had I not been strengthened by my Lord each step of the way. He was and is my strength and my peace in the storms I must face in life. Over time I have had to learn how to be content in every situation. I still have a long way to go in that department. Was I happy in the storm of watching my daughter slowly deteriorate and die at the age of twenty-six? Of course not. Did I have a choice; no I did not. God doesn't promise to take the storms of life away, but He does promise to guide you through the storm equipped with His peace, strength, and ability to go onward. So, take the next step, and another one trusting Him to be by your side holding your hand.

Some storms are of our own making. Every day we sin, but often without apology or remorse. Sometimes we don't even know we've caused a storm in someone else's life. When we come to see we have caused heartache or hurt, we should take steps to restore whatever was affected. That's easier said than done. If only we would be less worried about man's reactions, and more concerned about what God wants us to do. He says in Matthew 18, if someone has sinned against you, go to them and be reconciled. Basically, God wants us to work towards restoration in all of our relationships-first to God, then towards others. One step of faith may result in a changed life. Trust the Lord to be there each step of the way. Talk to Him much, asking for help, and wisdom, and He will direct your next step.

Step by step, one day at a time. Life can be downright hard sometimes. The world is not going to change, but you can with Christ's help. Daily we need the Spirit to be our guide and comforter as we endure the deep and sometimes extremely dark valleys. Relationship struggles, health issues, church disagreements, and job troubles. Where will you turn when the next storm hits? The Lord is waiting for you to ask Him to take your hand. He won't force you. Let Him lead you step by step through the dark and raging storm into the calm and peaceful light. No storm is too rough for Him, no problem more than He can handle. With Christ in my vessel, I can even smile in the storm. I know who can lead me on, take the burden of life's trials and heartaches and make them seem less. His name is Jesus. He won't let me go, He's going to walk with me and talk with me, and someday, lead me safely home to heaven.

There is one memory I wish to leave with you before ending this chapter. Over the past year, through the ups and downs of life, my Lord has brought one specific Bible story back to me over and over again every time I begin to fret. Jesus had been busy all day teaching and ministering to the crowds of followers. He had just fed the five thousand. He was probably very tired. Jesus made His disciples get in a boat and go before Him to the other side. Jesus then went off to pray. By evening, the boat with the disciples in it was in the middle of the sea. As you may have guessed, a storm crashed upon them with its vicious winds. The disciples were potentially in great danger. They were probably sure they were going to die. Jesus appeared, went to them, walking on the sea. He spoke to them calming their fears. He said, "Be of good cheer; it is I; do not be afraid" (Matthew 14:27). Peter then asked to come to the Lord, and then he did something amazing, he walked on water. This next part is what Jesus keeps bringing to my mind and heart. As we are amazed at what Peter was able to do, we are sad at the next moment as we read of Peter, suddenly realising and remembering the storm raging beneath his feet...begins to sink. Jesus thankfully came to his rescue, but also gently rebuked Peter for his lack of faith. The Lord can and will take us through the storms of life no matter how awful they seem. Ask Him to help you believe this truth. If we fix our eyes on Him, and not the storm, He will take us step by step through each and every trial in this life. Take His hand today, and as you fix your eyes on Him, stop and take note of how awesome it is to actually walk on water.

Notes

He has shown you O man, what is good; and
what does the Lord require of you but to do
justly, to love mercy, and to walk humbly with
your God.
Micah 6:8

7

Learning while Serving

I find it a nice treat to be invited to a party, wedding, or even go out for lunch once in a while with a good friend. As soon as you arrive, the waiter or happy hostess begins treating you like a visiting king or queen, making it their business to make your time more comfortable. It makes us feel cared for when someone else takes over and caters to your every need, doesn't it? No work, no dishes, and no clean up afterwards. You may even be treated extra special for a period of time. Ah, now there's something I must admit, I really enjoy once in a while.

What about when you are the one having the party, wedding, or special occasion at your house, or when the responsibilities for the occasion falls on you? Do you thrive on serving others, or do you tend to grumble with all the extra work needing to be done to ready yourself for this occasion? Serving others can be taxing; much energy is needed to complete all the necessary preparations. Catering to the needs of others is not a simple thing. It's a sacrifice of your time, energy, and even money.

As Christians we are called by God Himself to serve others (Galations 5:13, 1Peter 4:10). Serving others is really serving God. It says in Colossians 3:23, "Whatever you do, do it with all of your heart, as working for the Lord, not men. If you are a believer in Christ, you serve in response to all the Lord God has done for you. Serving God and others is how we show our thankfulness for all God is and has done, and is still doing in our lives.

If we want to know how to serve, we can begin by taking a closer look at how Jesus served. First, our Saviour was born into this sin-filled world so we could receive the good news. He lived among sinful people and yet did not sin. That's what I call a sacrificial life. Why did He do this? Jesus came to this earth so the Father's sovereign will could be carried out, and people would come to see their need of a Saviour. Christ became poor so you and I could be rich (1Corinthians 8:9). Jesus constantly put the needs of others before Himself. Look at how the New Testament mentions, several times, how Jesus was tired and even headed off to pray by Himself, and then we're told how the crowd approached Him again(read many passages in Matthew and Mark). Did Jesus say to Himself or others what a pain it was to not have some well-deserved rest? No, He demonstrated to His disciples how there is a time when we are to put our needs aside for the sake of others, especially when they show interest in knowing about God.

How often do you and I give of our time and energy to help in a difficult situation and do it totally without any grumbling at all? Hmmm, I would venture if you struggle like I do, then we tend to be much more like Martha in the Bible than Mary. I like to give to others, but usually on my time schedule. I also enjoy having friends over, but often struggle with whether I will have enough time to do everything before they arrive. If we are hospitable, how are we doing behind the scenes? Do you still look forward to the serving as much as the socializing, or does the socializing make the serving worthwhile?

Maybe our bad attitudes about serving stem from the large amount of questionable commitments we already have. What sorts of activities are you involved with right now? If you are convicted to serve more, and think of yourself less, it may not be quite as simple as just doing it. Prayer needs to come before making decisions, even ones with which we are sure the Lord would agree. Take a look at what you do, maybe write it down and categorize it: God, family, church, work, and community. How are you involved in each of these categories? Now ask yourself a hard question. Which of these things would God truly want you to participate in? Here's an example: I am a wife and mother, and so there are many sacrificial jobs I must do for my husband and children. Okay, but even here there can sometimes be a need for a repentant heart as complaining comes so naturally. The Lord God promises to help those who have a heart to serve. Trust Him and then do your daily jobs with a cheerful, content spirit. He will bless you back, even if you don't see it right away. A short verse I learned years ago comes to mind here....."Godliness with contentment is great gain" (1Timothy 6:6)

Don't forget your extended family. I know, we are busy people, especially if we have children. It may come easier if you tentatively write it on the calendar once a month to either call or visit. If family live close by, it might be convenient to pop over on the way home from church every few weeks. Invite them for supper once a month, or plan a get-together for a meal on birthdays and special events. Relationships with family are important to maintain.

81

If we are not careful, time flies and we can get used to not having them in our lives. This is sad, but true. We lived a couple hours away from our parents, so we planned right from the start of our marriage to go see them once a month. We didn't have a car for the first few years of our marriage, so had to take buses and trains to get there. When we had kids (and a van), we still went every month and called almost every week. It was a sacrifice of our time, energy, and money, but well worth it. As our parents have passed away, we have no regrets. If your family lives far away, try calling every two weeks or so, and if at all possible, plan to visit a few times a year for a few days. Grandparents love contact with their grandchildren, and with their grown children too. If it really isn't possible to visit them, at least encourage your children to make pictures, cards, and gifts to send. Phone or text them often just to keep the connections alive. Write a newsy letter every three months. I still send my one aunt a letter once or twice a year bringing her up to date on our family's doings. When I actually sit down and write, I am surprised at how little time it takes. Serving is worth the time it takes.

Next, comes church. Are you able to help in any way in your own family's church? If you are a busy mom at home, you may only be able to do small things to help out for now. Maybe you can pray for the families in your church, and call a widow once a month. When our kids were young, I took them to the nursing home to visit the elderly once in a while. Sometimes we took our pet rabbits, and once or twice we even took my son's pet pigeon. The people in these homes usually love anyone to visit and show they care. Two or three of my children have on occasion played their instruments for our church's Seniors Christmas meal. They loved it. I helped out for two years with a card ministry to the elderly. I could do this easily from my home. What about inviting a single from your congregation over for tea or lunch on Sunday once in a while? If we don't plan to at least try, then we will never end up changing anything. If you don't know what to help with at your church, ask the leadership, or one of the older people in the congregation.

Then there's work. Whoever goes to work in your household will most likely be around others. Maybe you both have to work. As believers, we are called to serve in whatever we do. Do you see your work as a service to God and others? Our attitude and our tongue portray strongly who we serve. Are we courteous or demanding, giving or selfish? Would others believe you if you told them you serve God and desire to give of yourself to others at your workplace, or would they say you are like all those other hypocrites who don't practice what they preach? How are you a witness for the Lord Jesus Christ in your work? No matter how unimportant you think your job is in the big scheme of things, it does matter how we serve while in it. God sees all things (Psalm 139), and His desire is to see His servants living and speaking for Him wherever they work. Be fair and truthful in all of your dealings with people. Pray you can live out Micah 6:8 which says, we are to act justly, love mercy, and walk humbly with our God. Commit each day to Him, and ask for opportunities to serve in your workplace. You never know what He may use to plant seeds of hope in someone's heart.

Your community is where you live, or the nearby town or city. How are you seen in this place? Do they see you or your family as part of them, or are you only a customer who frequents their stores and nothing else? Serving means looking for ways to give to others of your time, talents, and energies. When you walk through the stores, banks, post offices, and other places of employment, do you know the people's names who serve you on a regular basis? Do you attempt to make conversation with the workers in these establishments? Even short talks in a grocery store or bank can show people you care. Learning names, asking questions, and even smiling gives people the idea that you want to talk to them and even enjoy their company. Before you know it, witnessing in seemingly small ways can take place all because you took the time to serve them a small dose of God's caring and sharing. People remember others who pay attention to them. Many of my little experiences in the town where we live have come about, I believe, because God used my desire to serve right here. No, I am not involved in many community events since my kids have grown, but the people in town know I like living here. If the owners in the various stores you frequent were asked about you, what would they say? What did people say about Jesus? Be a witness wherever you go. Maybe you are uncomfortable speaking about the Lord with strangers, but your words and actions speak louder than you think. Remember, if we are Christians, we are ambassadors for Christ (2 Corinthians 5:20).

I like to encourage people. Learning people's names and making small talk is one way I show I care. Slowly over time, I ask questions about how they are, how they spend their time, and even ask about their desires in this life. Sometimes on my way into stores, I find myself praying for these opportunities. These opportunities are relatively short, but over a long while, I do see progress. There have been times when I've given people cards of encouragement and have even on occasion given a devotional book. I don't always have time to sit down for coffee, or attend events, but I do have time on occasion to make or buy cards and books to aid others in thinking about our Lord. He has blessed me back in this desire to serve. Serving others can be rewarding.

Jesus served those in need. Many times Jesus served those who were undeserving and seen as the worst people. What about some of the people in the Bible? There were the lepers, or the demon-possessed people, or the ladies with questionable reputations. They were the untouchables in those days. Jesus treated them the same as anyone else, with love and concern. It is so easy to serve those who will someday repay us, but how often do we reach out to those who are unfriendly, or don't pay us any attention at all? If we look around, I'm sure we can find people who would be described as untouchable, or undesirable. It helps to look at Christ. He showed us His love in that when we were still sinners, He died for us (Romans 5:8). Now that's true service. Ask the Lord to show you how to serve even the least of these. I'll be honest with you; I struggle with this one.

Once a month, on a Sunday evening, our family would go together to the local nursing home to participate in our church's service there. I must admit, by Sunday evening I'm pretty tired and not really wanting to go out again. I'd try to remind myself that I have always enjoyed conversing with the elderly. Usually, I ended up going. For many Sundays, this one lady attended, and you heard her before you even saw her. She was loud, barking out her hard to understand commands. At first, I admit, I avoided her; she literally scared me. Then the Lord nudged my heart. I said "hi" to her one month, and she barked back a hello to me. The next month, I tried to talk a bit to her asking if she liked the service. As time went on, I felt more at ease, and eventually caught her smiling at me. One night, I commented on her beautiful smile, and that caused a twinkle in her usually angry looking eyes. After one of the services, she barked out to me how she heard what the speaker had said. I patiently questioned her, and she barked back at me as I guessed her words wrongly at times. Finally, I understood. This interesting lady had heard the message of the gospel, her need to repent, and she now knew she was a sinner. My heart soared. I then asked her if she would like me to help her pray and tell Jesus she was sorry, and she said yes. I felt teary with joy. By the time I said amen, she too looked teary, but smiled the biggest smile. I told her she was now a child of God, and my sister in Christ. What a blessing! And to think, I nearly decided she was unreachable-how dare I! A fairly long while later, I heard she had passed away. Imagine if I had listened to my fears and ignored her barks. I learned a big lesson that evening. God will use those people who yearn to learn about serving Him and others.

Are you learning to yearn to serve as you grow in Christ? We are on this earth to live for God's glory, and to love our neighbour. This is our Christian service as it states in the beginning of Romans 12. It is small compared to what the Lord Jesus Christ has done for us. Are we willing to make our lives count for Christ, or will we go through this life always waiting to be served by others? I think you know the answer by now. Enjoy serving others, and pray the Lord helps you to learn more as you do.

Notes

Whatever you do in word or deed, do all in the name of the Lord Jesus, giving thanks to God the Father through Him.
Colossians 3:23

8

Learning to Focus on the Two Greatest Things

If I were to pose the question, "What are the two greatest things you are to do in this lifetime," how might you respond? Maybe you would strive to be the hardest, most dependable worker, or the best parent, or maybe become a world traveler, a famous writer, a mountain climber, or simply achieve a useful degree, get married and have a family. Wait a minute. Let's think about this. I said the greatest things you need to do, not the greatest you might hope to do. Does this change your answer?

I believe everyone has aspirations which they hope will fall into place somehow, even if we haven't told anyone. These desires begin to take shape while we are still children, and may grow to become a reality as we move through the years. Other ideas develop as we mature, work, and deal with everyday life. Our life experiences often mould what we hope to achieve here on this earth.

For example, if I had been abused as a child, I may head

in the direction of compassionate care to those who have suffered under similar conditions. Maybe I am attracted to children and books, so would hope to explore the idea of being a teacher or librarian. If my family experience was filled with loving and caring times, I may strive to repeat this with my own family. Being left out and lonely growing up may steer me in the direction of helping others feel loved. Sometimes what we end up gravitating towards is totally opposite to our background. Maybe I simply want a good, stable job and family to come home to, so I'll never be alone. Everyone has goals and hopes for their life.

What about when we devote our lives to following what the Lord God says? If the Lord has worked in our heart by His Spirit, does this change our life goals? I would say yes for the most part, but also no depending on what those goals are. If your goal is to honour and obey the Lord, then your thoughts, words, and deeds will strive to coincide with those desires. You will want your life to be a witness so it will glorify or lift up the Lord to others. If your goals are self-orientated, then eventually the Spirit will convict you, and you will want to change for His sake. Take a look at how you spend your days and why you do the things you do.

The Bible says the two greatest things I should strive to do in this life are to love God and love my neighbour as myself (Mark 12:29-31). Each of the gospels in the Bible repeats these two greatest commandments. Repetition of a phrase in the Bible tends to signify importance. The Old Testament states the Ten Commandments, and if we look closer at them, we will agree that they display God's command for us to love Him and our neighbour. Notice how the first four commandments are to do with loving God, while the last six with our actions towards our neighbour.

The Lord God of the universe created people to have a relationship with Him, and with each other. The Bible shows us over and over again what happens if we choose not to love God and our neighbour. Many stories in the Bible teach us about relationships. Read about Cain and Abel, Joseph and his family, Jacob and his wives, David and Bathsheba, and more. Our sinful nature causes relationships with God and others to be a constant battle (Romans 7). I'll be honest, I don't always want to do what God wants, which is showing my love for Him by my thoughts, words, and deeds. It is not always a simple task to be loving and kind to my family, friends, church, and community. My own selfish heart gets in the way. Daily happenings creep up on us where a conscious choice needs to be made: to keep striving to love God, and my neighbour, or go my own way. I need to pray for the Holy Spirit to guide me in these areas. Do you struggle with these issues too?

In my day-to-day life I am given tons of little ways in which I can either show God and my neighbour love, or follow my own desires. In my daily routine, I can choose to read my Bible to learn more about the Lord, or I can find other things to occupy my time. Excuses seem to flow so naturally as to my poor choices. For instance, I can run the little errands my family needs done, or let them find time to do them themselves. One thinks of others, the other only my time. When someone complains about the way I did or said something, I can either fling nasty, defensive words back, or accept the comment humbly and seriously. When I hear news about someone in difficult trials, I can decide to pray and look for ways to possibly reach out, or talk about it to others and not offer my help. My thoughts can be selfish, or Christ-centered. When I converse with others, I look towards the interests of others, or keep the focus on myself. Basically, just about everything I do, think, and say is either for God and my neighbour, or to please my own selfish heart.

Looking at my life this way is very convicting (and humbling), but daily examination by God's standards is necessary and helpful in my walk with Christ. It reminds me of my need of Christ and His work in my heart. Living for God is not easy, but when I remind myself of what He has done for me, then I am much more willing to give of myself. The closer I stay to the Lord and His word, the easier it becomes to live for Him. Read the book of Proverbs, and pay attention to God's wisdom spelled out for us in so many different scenarios. The Bible is never too old to speak to our lives.

Loving God comes by faith, and faith comes from hearing the message (Romans 10:17). We need help every day to learn and grow in our love for God. When the Lord God works in our heart, we begin to have a fervent longing to love Him back for His amazing grace and mercy extended to us through Jesus Christ. Our sin suddenly becomes exposed when we pay attention to Christ's overflowing love in His death for us, while we were still sinners. He has sent His Holy Spirit as a Helper to dwell within His people to equip them to daily make godly decisions (John 14:16-17). Reading and meditating upon the scriptures, and praying without ceasing seems the only way I've come to experience the closeness necessary to aid me in doing what is right in God's eyes. This is how we strive to live for His glory (Psalm 119, Joshua 1:8).

God knows who loves Him. He also knows when we are not doing well at loving Him. Several times in the New Testament, it states that Jesus knew their thoughts. He also tells us in Matthew how to love...unconditionally, as the Lord loves us, with a forgiving, humble, tender heart, with kindness, patience and unselfishness, and always seasoned with gentleness and self-control. That's quite the list of spiritual fruit, but one which the Lord says we possess if we are a believer in Christ. The old has gone, the new has come. In Christ, we are a new creation, we no longer live as we once lived (Galations 2:20). That's a very high calling and only possible through Christ. We will spend our life learning to fight sin, while learning to yearn to live for the One who gave His all for us.

Read the books of Ephesians, Colossians, Philippians and James. These are just a few of the Bible books in the New Testament which instruct us how we ought to live as believers in the Lord. Living for the Lord means we will want to show Him our gratitude in our day to day walk. When we struggle with displaying even one of these spiritual fruits listed in 1 Corinthians 13, it affects our relationship with God and with others. When the Lord brings to our attention a struggle with our relationships, do we ignore it, or do we seek to work on our own part of the problem?

For example, over the years the Lord has uncovered my fear of rejection. If someone is upset with me, it really bothers me to the point of making me an emotional mess. Because of this, I have tended to be overly quick to say sorry, even if it wasn't my fault. I never truly understood the reason until about three years ago. The Lord began to convict me of my apologies being at times quite superficial. It's not that I wasn't sorry the conflict had happened, but I think I wanted a quick resolution, where everybody was happy again. This was understandable, but wasn't true reconciliation. More recently, I have found the Lord convicting me more quickly, and when I apologize now, I am often humbled and able to take ownership for my part in the problem. I have also come a ways in the art of gentle confrontation when the fault is not mine, although still struggle with some fear. Sometimes our background history can make change difficult. Pray that the Lord helps you overcome your fears.

Pride can also be a big factor in holding us back from seeing our sin. It can be very difficult to own up to our faults. Ask the Lord to give you a tender spirit. Just think, if everyone treated each other with God's type of love, imagine the difference it could make in this world! It is important to state here, that without His Holy Spirit working within your heart, you will never truly be able to live as children of light. We often forget this, and figure we just need to work more diligently on our issues. Actually, we need His work in us every moment of the day. Pray for His love to overflow into your heart, and lead you to love Him more than yourself.

Sadly, our world today strongly suggests that we do not need God or His word anymore. We only need to look around us, and listen to the news to view the massive evidence everywhere of the world's rejection of God and His ways. Look at where these thoughts and actions have led us: to be haters of God, steeped in rampant sexual immorality, foolishness, wickedness, deceit, murder, loneliness, sadness, and sickness. Are these tragedies really God's fault, or have things just worsened because of people's selfish strivings?9 Do we think we can reject God and have no repercussions? I must mention there will always be some terrible atrocities beyond our comprehension.

Our world in general does not want to be led by the King of the universe, but I wonder if maybe at this point in history some may admit that our society is in one big, huge mess. Some blame the government, and others may try to blame certain races or religions. Sometimes, when tragedies occur, people even shake their fists at God. We don't want to confess He is in control especially when everything appears to be out of control. Remember, even when we don't understand, God promises to work things together for good, for those who love God and are called according to His purpose (Romans 8:28). Did you notice I said for those who love God?

Those who love God are assured of His working good in their lives, even if they can't see or understand it now. God never lies. He doesn't like the terrible situations taking place around us either, but promises to work them together for good for those who love Him. There are Christians all over the length and breadth of this world who will tell you how the Lord God has taken some of the most horrible trials in their lives and worked them for good somehow. For example, Joni Eareckson Tada is a woman who has been paralysed for most of her life due to a diving accident in her teens. For years now she has been a well-known speaker and author on the topic of trusting the Lord through suffering. If you read her books, you will be amazed at how this suffering saint has fervently served for God's glory since her terrible accident. So, you may wonder, do I now believe it was a good thing that my twenty-six year old daughter died of brain cancer? No, of course not. I don't think I will ever be able to say it was good that my daughter passed away at such a young age, but I have seen how her tragic death has opened several doors to talk about Christ with people in our sphere of influence. Then there's the wonderful development which took place over the next months. Our son-in-law fell in love with my middle daughter, and they are now happily married. My son-in-law and my grandson stay in our family, and my precious daughter is blessed with a godly husband. Many prayers have been answered there. This is what I'd call a blessing through hardship.

Do you see God's blessings amidst hardship? Do I pretend to understand God's workings? No, but that's okay. The Lord asks me to trust Him with all of my heart and lean not on my own understanding, but to acknowledge Him in all my ways, and then He promises to direct my path (Proverbs 3:5-6). I have learned firsthand what it means to totally depend on the Lord God to strengthen me moment by moment through the roughest times in life. Interestingly, I no longer seem as fearful in life's potentially stressful predicaments. In general, He has proved more times than I can count that He is my Rock, Refuge, and strength in circumstances I never believed I could possibly endure. My Lord has taught me to receive every day as a gift and not to take any for granted. Maybe you have experiences where God has used tough situations to teach you to depend on Him more. We can learn to be thankful for the good which comes from heartache and trial. God's grace can make you appreciate and love Him all the more. Are you willing to be taught through the storms in life? If you have a moment, look up Laura Story and her song "Blessings", and Casting Crowns and their song, "Praise Him in the Storm." These songs and others speak to how I feel about the storms in my life now.

Loving God is a lifelong process. Without Him you are lost, so go to Him and ask Him to work in your heart and life. Seek Him now whether you are in the worst storm of life, or even if you are enjoying a time of breathing easy. It's the most important thing you must do.

Loving your neighbour as yourself is a result of loving God. Jesus used the story of the Good Samaritan in Luke 10 to illustrate God's instruction to love your neighbour as yourself. In this story, a lawyer wanting to test Jesus asked Him what he needed to do to inherit eternal life. Jesus, knowing his thoughts, asked him to respond to the question according to his knowledge. The man knew the correct answer which was to love God with our whole being, and to love our neighbour as our self. Jesus responded by telling the lawyer that if he did these two things, he would inherit everlasting life. I believe we can be just like this man. He knew the right way to live, but then proceeded on to ask for further clarification. It says he, wanting to justify himself, asked, "Who is my neighbour?" Proudly, we can assume we are living our lives fairly well, and just need to learn a few pointers before we are all prepped for heaven. Was this man looking for a way out of loving his neighbour? Were there certain times in which not loving our neighbour was ok? God shows this man the answer through a story.

When Jesus tells stories, it appears He is attempting to have us ponder our own hearts in some respect. For example, the priest and Levite in this story show us that, even if we hold godly positions, we can still struggle with making huge errors in judgment and in loving others the way Jesus loves us. Even as people of God, we can easily assume someone else will do the dirty work. In all honesty, we don't like to get involved with messy situations, and sadly, most of the time would rather avoid sacrificing our time and energy. Sometimes, we actually go out of our way, like the "godly" men crossing the road," to stay out of any involvement. The Good Samaritan was the man who stopped to help the one hurt and lying on the ground. This suffering person is the same man left to die by the priest and the Levite. The Good Samaritan was the least likely to stop, and yet he does. He helps, he gives, and then he goes way beyond what most would even contemplate. This is just like what Jesus does for us. Read about it in Luke 10 to get the whole picture. Jesus then told the lawyer that he should go and do likewise. What can we learn from Jesus' story of the Good Samaritan? Are you ready, willing, and able to go out of your way for the next person you see in need? God says to love your neighbour as yourself.

This reminds me of one weekend when my husband, children and I had travelled to Toronto to visit extended family. We were on our way home and it began to change from rain to sleet. Suddenly, the busy highway became very slippery and quite slushy. As we carefully continued to drive along with the large crowd of vehicles, we became aware of cars suddenly sliding off of the side of exit ramps, and still others changing lanes and ending up right off the road. This comfortable ride had changed to one of danger. My husband and I noted a car up ahead sliding off the road and ending up in a shallow ditch. With my husband being a doctor, I wondered what his thoughts were at that very moment. Next thing I knew, our car was purposely, yet with great care pulling off the highway. I must admit, I was frightened for him, and for us as cars continued to zoom past. Looking somewhat scared himself, my brave husband basically crawled out of our van and then made his way haltingly over to the ditch. I prayed fervently for his safety, and ours too sitting at the side of the slippery highway. Our kids thought their dad was crazy and weren't afraid to voice it. In a few short moments, he returned, opened the trunk and closed it again. When he returned the second time, he breathlessly explained his activities since exciting the van. The driver of the ditched car was fine, and they had already called for help. My husband had returned for our emergency blanket, so he could aid their comfort while waiting. How many people do you know who would stop and take the same risk? As we sat there waiting, probably hundreds of cars zoomed past most likely commenting to one another of there being a car in the ditch. Maybe they even noticed the family who had stopped.

How can you be a good neighbour? Your first thought should be to ask yourself if you know Jesus Christ as Saviour? If the answer is no, then you must seek the Lord first. Loving your neighbour in a true and real way only comes from loving God. His love will overflow into you, and then to others. If you already love the Lord, then my advice is to study the life of Jesus, and research what the Bible teaches on relationships. God does not leave us without resources. He sends His word and Spirit to help and guide us. Pray for discernment and open eyes to see and know where you may be able to reach out and come to the aid of others. Sometimes the needs which appear will seem very small and insignificant in your eyes, but not to the person needing help. Pick up a fallen grocery item for an elderly person, or hold a door for a mom with children. Be alert to little things which can open doors to smile and be a light of Christ to others. Other times you may find you are wading into difficult and uncomfortable circumstances to be of assistance. Pray for courage and a willing heart. It may call for a sacrifice in some shape or form. Are you ready to really love your neighbour?

God says in Ephesians 1 that He has given us all we need for life and godliness. If we are believers in Christ, we have every spiritual gift necessary for life. The scriptures are our guidebook, and the Spirit applies what we need to our hearts. We do need to pray for a willing heart, to be taught, and then, even more to obey what is then understood to be right. Lots of Christians know how they should love according to God, but to follow through and do it is another issue all together. Try to remember, it is the second greatest commandment we are to live by.

Jesus was willing to come to this earth and suffer and die, so that we might live. He is our example, and He is the reason we can love others. There are two great commandments we must strive to live by in this life: to Love the Lord God with all your heart, soul, strength, and mind, and love your neighbour as yourself. He will teach you to love others the way His life reflects what is good and right. May the Lord bless you in striving to learn to focus on these two great commands.

Notes

Nevertheless we, according to His promise, look for new heavens and a new earth in which righteousness dwells. Therefore, beloved, looking forward to these things, be diligent to be found by Him in peace, without spot and blameless
2 Peter 3:13-14

9

While We Wait

Way back, when I was a little girl, I lived in the big city of Toronto, Ontario. I vividly remember my brother and I traveling to the bank with my mom every Friday after school. It must have been a popular time to cash or deposit your cheque, because there were always long line ups for my mom to stand in. My brother and I were sent to wait patiently on the big, black leather chairs. Sometimes for over an hour, we would count ceiling tiles and people in the line ups, and of course watched the numerous men and women receive their cash. We were usually bored after a bit and tired of waiting. Sometimes after what seemed like a decade, we would approach my mother, only to be sent back to our waiting place.

As I grew up, I learned that waiting was part of everyday life. Waiting for my teachers to start their lessons and waiting in line ups at grocery stores were common occurrences in my week. After accepting a job a fifteen to twenty minute car ride away from my home, waiting for city buses became the norm.

Everyone has to wait in some way. We'd probably be somewhat surprised if we counted all the minutes each day we wait for something or someone.

How do you wait? Are you a patient person while waiting? From my experience as a mother of seven children, I daily noticed their lack of patience. When small, they would tug on my pants, raise their little voices, and sometimes stomp their feet to let me know they were tired of waiting. I too, as a mom struggled to be patient with them. As we grow up, and want to have good relationships in this world, we accept that better behaviour is expected. No one likes to deal with impatient people.

It is difficult to wait, isn't it? Even in this technological era, it seems adults and young people are still playing the waiting game. If we are not texting, emailing, or messaging someone, we tend to be waiting for a reply. Over the years, many gadgets have made their way into our homes which supposedly help us save time and wait less. I'm not so sure they have done their job. I wonder if all these pieces of equipment have achieved is to make us more impatient, especially if they do not work the way we figure they should.

I text one of my children and sometimes they don't text right back. This may well and fine, but then I wonder after a short while, whether I wrote something in a manner that may have upset them, or were they just busy? Maybe they turned off their phone and forgot to turn it back on again, or maybe they are in class or driving somewhere. The longer they take, the more I might begin to fret. Are they ok? Maybe you think I'm being silly. What if the response is needed for with an anticipated visit or appointment? With texting, we get used to instant results. There have also been times when my husband has left for the hospital in bad weather to see his patients. As he leaves, he reassures me by saying he will call me when he arrives, but then in his busyness, forgets. I'm left to wonder if all is ok.

What about waiting for results from a blood test, or MRI because of a health issue? Many times over the years I've had various tests taken and had to wait days for the results. It's not easy to wait, but in most cases we have no choice.

When my husband, before we were married, went to university in London, Ontario, I was still attending school and working in Toronto. We were apart for two full school years, seeing one another only every few weeks. Waiting for him to come home was a struggle, especially when it stretched out to four to six weeks in his second year. I missed him. To bridge the time when we would see each other next, we wrote many letters, and made lots of late Saturday evening calls. Throughout this separation, we still had to show patience while anticipating the next call or letter to arrive.

God says patience is a fruit of the Spirit, something which develops as we mature in our relationship with Him (look at Galations 5:22-25 and 1 Corinthians 13). Hopefully over time you can say you have grown in being patient. If you are growing in patience, it will be a witness to those around you of God's work in your life.

How about waiting on the Lord? Are you like most people and find it tough to wait for the answer to your prayers? Many times in the Bible, God encourages us to trust and wait on Him. Thankfully, He also gives us encouragements in His word to help us wait. His promises can help us believe He will answer (Psalm 34:40). David was a man who openly tells us in several of the Psalms that he, too, struggled with waiting on the Lord. He asked the Lord more than once, "How long, O Lord?"(Psalm 13,

Habakkuk 1:12, Psalm 71:12). I will admit, I don't relish waiting for the Lord God to answer my prayers. We can be such impatient people.

Patience seems to grow more slowly in some of us. What will we do while we wait? Some keep busy; others pray. Both are good ideas. Others find they wrestle in their minds by stewing and imagining what will happen if the Lord doesn't answer soon, or if He will give an answer which wasn't what they requested. I must admit, for years I fell into the latter. In James 1, it instructs believers to count it all joy when we fall into various trials, for it produces patience. Does this mean we are to be joyful while hurting, or not knowing what is to come next?

Maybe the Lord has a reason for wanting us to wait, or maybe He has answered, but we aren't happy with what we see. The Lord desires to teach us to grow in our dependence on Him, especially during times of fretting over the unknown. I believe we are to expect answers, but also to be ready and willing to accept His will no matter what may come. God says He has a plan, and it is good (Jeremiah 29:11). This is sometimes extremely difficult to swallow. Some may come to the conclusion our Lord God is mean if He does not answer our prayers our way. It takes faith to believe that God's ways are right and good, even when they appear contrary to our own preconceived ideas. God tells us to trust Him with our whole life, and not lean, or depend on our own understanding. He promises He will guide our path if we do depend on Him (Proverbs 3:5-6).

Faith in the Lord is a process. We believe the basics of who God is, who we are, what God has done through Christ, and what that means for us now and into eternity. Over time, if we truly seek the Lord on a daily basis, we begin to learn much more about our amazing God. He has many things He wants us to know and believe, and tons of others facts we can learn and through them grow spiritually. The Lord God expects His children to live for Him and trust His ways are right. There are many verses and stories in the Bible which point to our need to trust in God. Stories like Cain and Abel, Noah and the ark, Abraham and Isaac, David and Goliath, and Daniel and the Lion's Den being just a few of the stories which show us what happens when we trust God, but also when we don't. They help us to understand why God says "no" sometimes, and why He wants us to live His way.

His word becomes our precious guidebook for life and prayer our lifeline of communication with our Father in heaven. His promises start to aid us in our daily walk as children of light, especially in times of trials and hardship. Lots of God's ways can still seem so very challenging to understand, but if we are wise, we will trust Him. The fear of the Lord is the beginning of wisdom (Proverbs 1:7). We study and depend on God to show us the way (Psalm 119, Psalm 1, Proverbs 3:5-6). Pray for the Lord God to give His Spirit to teach you all things (John 14). Ask Him to increase your faith.

At some point we may naively assume we have become pretty godly. This is a dangerous place to be. We might even wrongly figure we have God and His ways pretty well figured out. Beware of pride. There is always more to learn in this lifetime. With the Lord as our God and King, we are students in His classroom as long as we live. If you read Joshua 1:8-9, it advises us to not let God's truth depart from our mouth, but that we should have it constantly on our mind all the time. God promises us that if we do this, we will live prosperous and successful lives according to His will. In verse nine, Joshua (and you and I) are told not to fear, "for the Lord God is with you wherever you go." Joshua had been placed by God in a leadership role and would need God's presence and guiding hand. Verse eight and nine show us how God is preparing Joshua for what was ahead. The Lord prepares us too, if we are willing.

But what about when the real tests of life jolt us into realising our need of Christ every moment of the day? Trials and suffering like never before can hit you headlong when you least expect it. Suddenly you have to choose either to depend on the Lord, or push Him away. Are His promises true even when nothing else makes sense? What about when you have pressing questions for God as you trudge through the raging storms? "Why is this happening?" "Why isn't God taking care of me anymore like He promised?" Waiting for answers at times like these can become almost as overwhelming as the affliction you are facing. Over the years and seemingly at a snail's pace, I've been brought by the Lord to surrender my burdens to Him instead of holding on to them. He promises me the wisdom, strength, and peace to handle whatever comes. This in itself has been a long and sometimes painful process so far. I wish I had fretted much less and trusted more. Sadly, I have probably not always been the best example, being such a worrying mom and wife instead of trusting my gracious and ever providing Lord.

Learning to be patient with others and with the Lord's answers and timing takes much prayer and faith. Ask the Lord to show you in which areas you need to trust Him more, and how to go about this. God's word and Spirit will help you, and over time, if you have a willing heart, He will guide you in depending on Him. He desires that we ask Him for help. It can aid us to remember how patient God is with us in our walk with Him. Also, you can read in the book of Exodus and Isaiah how patient God was with the unfaithfulness of Israel time and time again. He does the same for us.

Believers also strive to trust and believe that someday the Lord Jesus will return. The New Testament is full of promises for both now, when He returns, and for eternity. Do we ever ponder what we should do while we wait for Him to return?

There are probably a myriad of ways in which we react to waiting for the Lord's return. Hopefully, you wait with anticipation. Think about some of the things I wrote about yearning for the Lord God. Ask Him to help you to yearn for Him while you wait. Longing for God will encourage you to stay close to Him while continuing to trust His timing to be right.

Reading about the Lord's return and pondering what it will be like to see my Saviour face to face should cause me to long for his return. When I see Him, my faith shall be sight, and the battle will be over: no more sin, no more sorrow, and no more pain. If I believe His precious promises given in His word, then when I die or meet the Lord upon His return, will I do so with a shout of joy? Will I be excited to finally begin eternal life forever with my Lord? How will you feel? Will you maybe be fearful of that great day? Do you worry about your standing with God when He arrives for His people? Your fear of His return makes sense, if you do not love the Lord God and have salvation through Jesus Christ. Also, if you know the Lord, but are not diligently living for Him in this life, you need to be reminded that everyone must give account of their life to the Lord when He returns. You will not be given a second chance after you die, or on that great day. Today is the day of grace; "Believe on the Lord Jesus Christ now, and you will be saved" (Acts 16:31). There is still time. You will find there is no other true salvation in any other. "Jesus is the way, the truth, and the life. No one comes to the Father except through Me" (John 14:6).

Some people may tire of waiting for the Lord's return and get involved in other things. Maybe they start to doubt God's promises, and wander away towards people and activities which they hope will bring true satisfaction and joy to them now. This will not last as it is temporal and fleeting. The devil would like to see us head in this direction. It is the broad road and leads to destruction. This is why we must stay focused on loving the Lord and our neighbour. Only God's truth has treasures which last forever. His word is helpful in all of life's joys and disappointments (2Timothy 3:16). Ask the Lord to open your eyes and show you where you may be wandering away instead of trusting Him. Stay close to God while you wait.

If we take our eyes off of the Lord, we will be more inclined to be tempted by our world, the devil and our own sinful heart to stray toward this world's treats and trinkets. We may believe we are satisfied for a time, but it is an illusion which will not bring us true and lasting peace or joy. Today's temptations may present itself wherever we spend our time, energy, and money. For instance, the internet may be a great tool for looking up a variety of different topics, but can also be a very dangerous temptation area for coveting, pornography, adultery, and many other eye-catching scenarios. Even reading and viewing all the many interesting events and entertaining items which scroll across our Facebook feeds each day can use up a lot of time. We can spend whole evenings on these sites without realising the concerns. Would you say everything you read or see on the internet is good for your soul? How would the Lord feel about this if He returned right now? It may be wise to pay attention to your leisure time.

For instance, Pinterest is a fun way I discovered to look up all sorts of topics on the Internet and save them to try later. When I first starting looking up various items such as recipes, verses, organisational ideas, marriage encouragements, and more, I found it was very enticing, and the time flew. After a few months, I was literally being drawn to that site where I enjoyed finding useful tools for my home. I believe there wasn't anything necessarily wrong with this new entertainment. Then one day, it dawned on me. I was at times wasting whole evenings on my computer on this particular site. No, I wasn't looking at "bad" things, but I began to wonder if maybe I should limit my time on this site. Since then, I try to only go on Pinterest in the evening hours, and if my work for the day is done. I also try to stay off of it when family or friends are around and attempt to limit my viewing time. For a while, I found I was feeling a bit bored, but then found other ways to spend my time.

Back to our thoughts on what to do while we wait for the Lord to return, or our day of death. There are those who have Christian teaching in their background who may begin to wonder if they should be doing more to bring the kingdom of God to fruition while they wait. This is not bad in itself, but we need to be very careful. The focus on Christ-centered thoughts, words, and deeds can so quickly change and become focused on what we can do and accomplish. Our time and efforts can become more man-centered instead of God-centered. We easily fall into the trap of following our own desires to be in control of the doing, instead of asking for wisdom and responding to our Lord and Master. I wonder if this is a temptation for all believers at some point. Pray to the Lord, and ask Him to keep you focused on what His plans are, not yours.

God has good works planned for those He has saved (Ephesians 2:10). Good works are the things God instructs us to do for Him and others, and they are our response to His working in our heart. Ask the Lord to make it clear to you what He'd have you to do today, tomorrow, and for the rest of your life. It says in James that faith without works is dead. I believe the Lord will show you the way when you commit yourself to His guiding hand. You might be surprised at what He has planned for you. When we figure we have our life planned out, we can end up disappointed when the unexpected happens. Pray for humility and wisdom as you are directed to what God wants you to do before He returns. Pray every day for the Lord to steer you to what He wants you to do. We think we know what we're going accomplish today, tomorrow, and next week, but have we even inquired of the Lord? Are these ideas God's, or ours? Writing about these topics convicts me. I like to plan ahead to do this or that, but do I actually pray and ask if this is the Lord's will for me?

How do we show our anticipation for the day when we meet the Lord face to face? Well, my personal response is, I hope to yearn for spiritual growth in seeking Him now, and be busy about living for Him in this life. I try hard not to think about what I may gain from it, but what will bring Him glory. My attention is brought to face the fact of how I often fail at being His faithful disciple. The world is watching us Christians, and what do they see? When the world looks at us, they should see Jesus shining through. There is still much work to be done: people who need to hear the gospel, verses to be shared, and definitely lots to still learn ourselves. I'm sure the Lord would hope to find us being faithful servants in His vineyard. What will the Lord God find you doing when He returns? Are you using the talents and gifts He graciously has given you to use for Him?

Now at this point, I feel the need to bring up a delicate subject, but one, I believe of great importance. All of us, being human, at some time or another in our lives have troubles or conflicts in our relationships. We at times clash and disagree with others throughout our day-to-day interactions. Here is the question to ponder: Are there any relationships in your life presently at odds? If the Lord was to return today, or if death suddenly ended any possibility of reconciliation with that person--will you wish you had worked more diligently to work things out? We are told in the New Testament to make every effort to make peace with our neighbour (Hebrews 12:14, Romans 12:18). In Colossians and Ephesians we are advised to take off bitterness and anger against others and replace it with forgiveness. If we have a problem with a person and it is affecting our lives, the Lord says in Matthew 18 to leave our gift at the altar and go make amends first. In my reading of this scripture, the impression is that we are to put our worship of the Lord God on hold for a time and work out the disharmony first. Wow! I'd say that means being at odds with a person also affects my relationship with God. Reconciliation is of paramount importance to the Lord. Remember as I've already shared earlier in the book, if we love God, loving our neighbour is the result which flows from this relationship. There are times when it appears too difficult to know how to remedy the conflicts which arise. Christ was willing to die for sinners, so that they would be reconciled to Him. So, while you wait, work on relationships.

This is a tough one, isn't it? None of us likes confrontation, but all of us like it when our relationships are loving and encouraging. I sometimes wonder if we maybe fear man more than God. Looking at the way the Lord has dealt with me and my sin helps immensely with my desire to work towards reconciliation with others. If He can forgive me, then I should be able to forgive others. Pray for the strength to do what needs to be done to

113

reconcile fractured relationships. This may mean going to counselling or getting outside help, if needed. Sometimes having an unbiased person hear both sides of the story can clear up preconceived notions. Remember, you may not have the gift of another day.

Forgiveness is a very important aspect in our life with Christ. God says if you confess your sins, He is faithful and just and will forgive and cleanse you from all unrighteousness (1 John 1:9). Do we desire our life to be right with God? Then repent and believe He forgives you. When we repent of our wrong ways, He gives us freedom, peace, and a stronger desire to extend forgiveness to others.

So, while you are waiting for Lord, are you also busy with good God-honouring activities? Like what you say? Well, do you honour the Lord in your work whatever that may be? Then ask yourself, "If I am a believer, am I a witness for the Lord in that place?" Are you acting, speaking, and thinking in a way which would please the Lord? Where do you spend your time outside of work? If we really think about it, we know which activities are not on God's list of places to be. Would God work somewhere where the job requires you to work on Sundays? Today, this is an issue for many. I'm not talking about nursing homes, or hospitals which are necessary helps needed for the sick and elderly. I'm talking about all the various factories and stores which do not need to be open on the Lord's day. Are you being asked at work to participate or advocate anti-Christian attitudes and beliefs? How would you describe the atmosphere at your work? Would the Lord work there? Would He be pleased to see what your workplace does, what you do?

Every day living like maintaining a home, taking care of children, going to various activities, and socialising as a

couple , family, or single are all God-honouring things to
participate in outside of work. I imagine most of you
wouldn't regret having a church family and worshiping
God on a weekly basis. Having a church family is very
special and can be a great support system especially when
you are going through tough times. I love the communion
of the saints; it encourages me in my walk with the Lord.
Church is not the only place to find God honouring
activities, but they can be very rewarding and enjoyable.
Try to get involved in a Bible study, and offer your services
teaching in some kind of outreach club, or even offering to
do some of the background work needed. Exercise and
sports are fun ways to stay healthy and connect with others.
Pick up the phone, and make contact with people in your
sphere of influence. It is well worth the effort to bless
others. Ask a friend out for coffee, drop over to someone's
house to bring some muffins you've just baked. Send a
card, or write a letter. Enjoy the life God gives you by
looking for some of the sweet opportunities He has
provided. Use your time and energies to serve Him right
where you are. If you are struggling with chronic health
issues and can't go out on a regular basis, ask the Lord to
give you ideas on where and how to serve Him right where
you are. Praying for others is a special service to others too.
Calling or emailing others with words of encouragement
can make someone's day even if it feels like such an
insignificant thing. The possibilities might be limited for
you, but ask the Lord what you can do today to serve Him
while you wait. Recently, I heard a story of an elderly lady
who had become too frail to play as the pianist for her
church. Apparently she had played there for many years.
Even though she couldn't go out much anymore, she
decided to advertise in the newspaper to play favourite
pieces of music for people over the phone. Apparently she

experienced many wonderful opportunities talking with others and blessing their lives. God uses those who are willing to be used for Him.

For example, maybe try to make time to visit widows and widowers; they truly are glad for the fellowship. If you are shy, then take a friend along with you. Be a light in this dark world; use your time wisely. In the Bible it says to use the opportunities in your life for good as the days are evil (Ephesians 5:16). Today people have such a tendency to waste a lot of hours watching movies, playing computer games, surfing the internet, scanning Facebook, and watching sports events. I'm not against these particular activities and even participate in some of them myself, but see how quickly whole evenings or weekends can disappear when we sit and stare at our screens every day while we could be doing something more constructive. Pray for the Lord to guide you in how to spend the days, months, and years He grants to you.

I've given several ideas in this chapter of what to think and do while waiting on the Lord. I hope this book has given you much to meditate upon concerning your life now, and the one which the Lord says is to come. While we wait, there will probably still be many storms to endure. Are you prepared to walk through them?

My hope is that you are beginning to learn to yearn for the Lord God. After reading this book, my prayer will be that you meditate and pray more about some of the topics introduced, and use them as reminders. Remember, only the Lord can help us yearn for Him while going through the many disappointments, hurts, and terrifying afflictions in this life. Storms will come, so be prepared. Stay close to the Lord, and keep learning. We truly can walk above the raging storms if our eyes are fixed on Him alone. Only Christ will give you the ability to walk on the water and safely reach the other side. His hand is open, and He is waiting for you to reach out to Him and start walking.

Notes

Notes

Now to Him who is able to keep you from stumbling, and to present you faultless before the presence of His glory with exceeding joy, to God our Saviour, who alone is wise, be glory and majesty, dominion and power, both now and forever. Amen.

Jude

Notes

Notes

88698812R00067

Made in the USA
Columbia, SC
09 February 2018